THE OTHER MIDLAND REDS

BMMO BUSES SOLD TO OTHER OPERATORS

1924–40

DAVID HARVEY

AMBERLEY

First published 2012

Amberley Publishing
The Hill, Stroud
Gloucestershire, GL5 4EP

www.amberley-books.com

British Library Cataloguing in Publication Data.
A catalogue record for this book is available from the British Library.

ISBN 978 1 4456 1329 1
Ebook ISBN 978 1 4456 1341 3

Typeset in 10pt on 12pt Sabon.
Typesetting and Origination by Amberley Publishing.
Printed in the UK.

Contents

Front Cover Images

Above: *44 (EH 4941)*
The first twelve SOS S types were actually built in 1924 by BMMO on Tilling-Stevens TS3 chassis and with one exception were fitted with Brush B32F bus bodies. This one is standing on Campbell Road near the Michelin tyre factory on 10 March 1925. The S types had a four-speed crash gearbox and the early use of pneumatic tyres enabled the performance to be very impressive for the time. EH 4941 was Potteries Motor Traction's fleet number 44, and remained in service until 1934. At the top of the steep trio of steps is the bulkhead window, which appears to have a fare table in it. And just look at the state of the mudflaps, reflecting the often poor condition of the roadsm even in the 1920s. (J. Cooke Collection)

Below: *1010 (RC 3332)*
Filling up with a good load in more or less the same place as 1012 some ten years earlier in Derby Bus Station is Metro-Cammell-bodied 1010 (RC 3332). These fifty-six-seater metal-framed bodied buses were well constructed and served as front-line vehicles in the Trent fleet for over fifteen years. It is working on the 12 route by way of Ockbrook, an ancient village 4 miles east of Derby and seperated from Borrowash by the A52 road. Ockbrook is most noted for its Moravian Church Boarding School, which was founded in 1750. The early post-war livery of all-over red was reminiscent of the Midland Red colours. The Trent vehicles had all the usual Midland Red idiosyncracies, with narrow cabs, a petrol tank beneath the driver's seat in the cab and the quaint suggestion of a vestigial piano-front just below the destination box. (R. F. Mack)

Rear Cover Image

339 (UP 552)
There were sixty-five SOS QLs delivered to Northern General during 1928 and all of them survived the Second World War. By now fitted with roof-mounted destination boxes, 339 (UP 552), one of the fifty-one Northern General QLs bodied by Brush, survived to become of the last nine remaining in service, lasting until 1950. The QL vehicles differed from the earlier Qs by having front-wheel brakes, easily identifiable by the disc-shaped front wheels. In addition, for the first time with an SOS design they were fitted with twin rear wheels. The tiny windscreen at the prow of the narrow cab was modified from earlier vehicles by having a deeper windscreen. (J. C. Gillham)

Acknowledgements

My sincere thanks are accorded to John Banks who has allowed me to use the wonderful photographs of the late Geoff Atkins, to Roger Carpenter, John Carroll, John Cook of the Potteries Enthusiasts Group, Robert Kell for finding a photograph of a Sunderland District bus, to Roy Marshall, the Northern General Group's archive, Harold Peers, the staff of the Peterborough Reference Library, Andrew Porter, Mike Rooum and Alan Wycherley for allowing me to use either their photographs or those in their ownership. Elsewhere, the photographs which are not credited on the print and therefore cannot be traced to a photographer are credited to my own collection of SOS bus photographs which I have built up over the last forty years.

I would also add that without my wife Diana's unstinting support and proof reading skills this book could not have been completed.

Introductory Background

At the time of writing there are just five pre-war SOS buses that were built for other operators that are preserved and another ten built for Midland Red, varying from running vehicles to derelict, but safely in store. This is not surprising as the buses all date from 1940 or earlier and are therefore at least seventy years old.

The task of finding and collecting photographs of each of the types with each of the companies who operated the SOS type buses has taken many years, and with the exception of the preserved Midland Red and Trent SONs, all the photographs are in black and white. This is not surprising as the last non-Midland Red SOS ran in about 1958.

At the time of writing there are only four types of bus that have not been traced with other operators. These are the 1927 SOS Qs of Llandudno Blue, of which there were five; the Potteries Motor Traction pair of QLC touring coaches of 1930; the four IM6 buses supplied to Sunderland District in 1931; and a pair of very late SOS IM4s supplied to Tynemouth & District in 1933. All others are accounted for and where possible more than one example of each type is illustrated. In addition, for each type of SOS bus or coach there is again at least one comparative photograph of the model in the parent Midland Red fleet.

Each type of SOS vehicle has its specification detailed in each section and this is followed by photographs of that chassis type, firstly with the Birmingham & Midland Motor Omnibus Company (better known as Midland Red). The bulk of each section is then taken up by those buses operated by the BET Companies that received SOS chassis, and this serves as the basis of this book.

A Brief Background to SOS Chassis Production by BMMO

The Birmingham & Midland Motor Omnibus Company began to operate motor buses in the Birmingham and Black Country area on 25 May 1912, using from the beginning petrol-electric Tilling-Stevens TTA1 and TTA2 models which were fitted with double-decker bodies. By 1914 the first thirty of these buses were sold to Birmingham Corporation Tramways when the famous 'Birmingham Agreement' came into effect, leaving the company with just seven double-deckers. This meant that the Corporation had the rights to operate their own buses within the Birmingham boundary, while Midland Red, as the company was beginning to be known, could radiate its services from Birmingham while concentrating on firstly developing its Black Country services and later taking on routes in Worcester, Tamworth, Kidderminster and even Leicester.

The buses purchased from 1914 and throughout the First World War were more Maidstone-built Tilling-Stevens TS3 petrol-electrics, but these normal-control buses were single-deckers. These buses were available to bus operators during the First World War around the country because their petrol-electric transmission was considered by the British Army too complicated to maintain in the battle areas in France and Belgium. Thus AEC and Daimler buses were impounded by the War Department as they had gearboxes and clutches whereas the Tilling-Stevens vehicles had a petrol engine driving a generator; this provides traction current to an electric motor which drives the bus. This is basically the same principle as a modern Diesel-electric railway locomotive. Ironically it was the very same petrol-electric transmission which made them easy for the bus drivers to master! The war-time single-decker buses delivered to Midland Red had lightweight bodies, seating between twenty-nine and thirty-two passengers, and were a great success, allowing the company to expand their operating area dramatically by about 1920.

Throughout the 1920s Midland Red buses were responsible for the closure of many tramway systems because of their relative speed and comfort in relation to the old, competing Edwardian tramcars. Yet the buses which inflicted this terminal damage to tramway systems in the Midlands were not the petrol-electric single-deckers built by Tilling-Stevens but buses developed by Midland Red's Chief Engineer Mr L. G. Wyndham Shire. Shire had realised in the early 1920s that in order to consolidate services, expand the area of operation and drive the associated BET tramway operators into extinction, he had to develop a new type of single-decker. Shire realised that the Tilling-Stevens petrol-electric chassis were too slow and were being outperformed by small independent operators' buses, especially in the Black Country, Worcester, North Warwickshire and Leicester areas.

The company purchased a pair of eleven-seater Model T Fords in 1921, while during the following year fourteen 20 hp Garfords imported from the USA were placed into service with a variety of bodies, ranging from fifteen to twenty-four seats. Mr Shire's report on these small, fast and lightweight buses, after extensive testing, was that although these specific chassis were something of a developmental 'dead end' they pointed the way forward amd as a result the company should build its own buses to his specification. Thus the SOS marque was born, with the letters standing for 'Shire's Own Specification'. The advantage of doing this was that the company could design exactly what it wanted without having to compromise its needs by adopting a vehicle from an outside manufacturer.

An important by-product of the decision to manufacture their own buses at Carlyle Road Works was that the company had the capacity to manufacture buses for other BET Group operators, with the Northern General group, Potteries Motor Traction and Trent Motor Traction becoming the most important customers up until just after the outbreak of the Second World War.

SOS Chassis Types New to Other Operators Built Between 1923 and 1940

Year	Chassis type	BMMO	Northern	Tyne mouth	PMT	Trent	Llandudno Blue	Ortona	Peterb.	Wakefields	Sunde land
1923	S	22									
1924	S	39	1		12		4		6		
1925	S	115	50		31	2	2	3	6		
	FS	1									
1926	S	4	10	6		30	4	4	3		
	FS	84			2						
	Q	1									
1927	S						2				
	Q	109	25	11	10	25	5	7	8		
	QC	14				5					
1928	QL	170	65	5	50	38	16		5		
	QLC	15	10			3	2				
	M	2									
1929	M	47	40		25	30	6	5	12		
	QLC	30									
	XL	50									
	COD	1									
	MM	39									
	IM4	1	1								
	ODD	51				21	6	5			
1930	MM	10									
	COD	22			21	17					
	QLC	18			2	3	2				

Year	Chassis type	BMMO	Northern	Tyne mouth	PMT	Trent	Llandudno Blue	Ortona	Peterb.	Wakefields	Sunder land
	RR	50									
	SRR	2	10								
	BRR	1									
	IM4 ex MM	38			1						
1931	IM4	51	10		13	12					
	IM6	22	10			16					4
	REDD	1									
1932	IM4	50			6	25					
	IM6	28				10				2	
	REDD	50			4						
1933	IM4	30				25					
	IM6		10								
	BRR	20									
	LRR	1									
	FEDD	1									

The First Generation of SOS Buses

SOS S Type

The first bus built by Midland Red to have the SOS name marque was the forward-control S type. The letters SOS were, according to a 1930 lecture on the development of Midland Red's 'in-house' buses by Traffic Manager Mr O. C. Power, the acronym for 'Shire's Own Specification', named after the Company's chief engineer, Mr L. G. Wyndham Shire. Shire's original design was a straight-framed, lightweight normal-control chassis fitted with a four-cylinder side-valve 4.344 litre petrol engine with Ricardo modified cylinder heads, a four-speed gearbox and an early use of pneumatic tyres. Developed from the last batch of Tilling-Stevens TS3s delivered in 1922, which by that time were being built with four-speed gearboxes, the first of the SOS S types actually had Tilling-Stevens TS3 chassis frames. The chassis was fitted with a radiator similar to those on the Tilling-Stevens buses but the SOS version was taller, straight-sided and with the legend 'MIDLAND RED' on the header tank. The chassis was fitted with a thirty-two-seat wooden-framed six-bay body and an all-up weight of 3¾ tons. The result was a neat, fast, reliable, lightweight single-decker with a better-than-average seating capacity that did everything to meet the company operating requirements and was more than a match for the contemporary single-deck buses used by competitors. For the first time, the driver sat over the fuel tank, which was mounted in the cab. By 1925 some 205 had been built, with 113 being used by BMMO.

The first year of production was 1923 and all the first twenty-two SOS S types were delivered to Midland Red, so that the first buses built for another operator were not placed in service until 1924. Between 1924 and 1926, Northern General bought sixty-one SOS S chassis, while the associated Tynemouth Company received six buses in 1926. Both of the North Midlands BET operators received the S type bus, with Potteries Motor Traction getting forty-three chassis between 1924 and 1925 while Trent Motor Traction had thirty-two with the last thirty entering service during the last year of manufacture. In East Anglia, Ortona of Cambridge received seven S types while Peterborough Electric purchased fifteen of these normal-control buses. In North Wales, Llandudno Blue received twelve S types, including the last two of the model to be built, which entered service in 1927.

BMMO

492 (HA 2431)

The ninety-seventh SOS chassis to be constructed was a Brush-thirty-two seater S type, HA 2431. This bus entered service in 1925. Its crew stand in front of their charge in the middle of Hereford near to the Old House in High Town when still quite new. The standard S type was a lightweight and fast single-decker and was instrumental in increasing the popularity of bus services operated by Midland Red. In so doing many smaller independent operators could not survive the competition, further increasing the dominance of the company throughout their large operating area. When operated by associated BET bus operators, the S type had the same effect. (C. Carter)

556 (HA 2491), 558 (HA 2494) (Above)
The bustle of Ashby-de-la-Zouch's Market Street in 1933 reflects the busy Leicestershire town. The three boys on their cycles are positively whizzing down the hill, passing the Leicestershire County-registered Wolseley Nine on the right and behind it a 1930 Austin 20 hp. Pulling away from the bus stand is SOS S type HA 2491. It is on the way to terminate in Station Road near to the former Midland Railway Station and to connect with the Burton & Ashby Light Railway, which was operated until February 1927 with open-topped double-decker trams when it was taken over by Midland Red. The Leicester to Burton upon Trent line opened in 1845 and was closed by British Railways in September 1964. Parked on the right is HA 2494, another of this Ransomes-bodied batch. Both of these thirty-two-seaters entered service in 1925 and would remain in service for another year. (S. L. Smith)

Northern General
S299 (PT 7233) (Opposite top)
The first SOS S types were basically modified Tilling-Stevens TS3 chassis fitted with four-speed crash gearboxes replacing the original style of petrol-electric transmission. Although there were three deep steps into the saloon, these were considerably lower than those on contemporary single-deckers. S299 (PT 7233) was one of the last S single-deckers to enter service not only with Northern General but with any of the other BET groups that were associated with Midland Red bus production. S299 entered service in April 1926 and its Brush B31F body is in its original condition, still carrying the quarter-covered rear mudguards. The bus remained in service until 1937, after which it ended its days as a caravan, a fate that befell many a pre-war SOS-built bus. (D. R. Harvey Collection)

209 (PT 4852) (Above)

One of the first SOS S type production vehicles was 209 (PT 4852), which had the BMMO chassis number 11. It entered service in March 1925 and had Brush-built B31F bodies built to Midland Red specification. After its first rebuild in about 1930, 209's chassis was rebuilt, fitted with front-wheel brakes and equipped with more substantial pneumatic tyres. At the same time the rocker panels were lengthened, all of which substantially altered and modernised the appearance of these early normal-control single-deckers. In this form 209 survived until 1938 and was scrapped in August of that year. (Courtesy Go Ahead Northern)

592 (HA 2440) (Above)
HA 2440 was a former Midland Red charabanc with a Davidson CH32 body, but was transferred to Northern General in 1927 as NGT 337. It was one of six SOS S types built in May and June 1925 and was transferred to Wakefields Motors, Tynemouth, in 1933 before returning to the main parent fleet just two years later as 592. 592 was one of two of these vehicles to be lengthened by the company in 1933 when it was rebodied by Short with a B36F body, making it resemble a lengthened SOS ODD. The radiator looked somewhat anachronistic, but despite this 592 survived until 1952, albeit being used mainly as a driver training vehicle. (Courtesy Go Ahead Northern)

Tynemouth & District

10 (FT 1385) (Opposite above)
The small Tynemouth & District bus fleet bought their first BMMO SOS chassis in 1926. They purchased six S types which lasted for nine years, being withdrawn in 1935. The Tynemouth SOS S types basically remained in this condition for the whole of their lives. The bus has slip boards for Whitley Bay, Seaton and Blythe. These neat little buses were instrumental in expanding the bus service on the north bank of the River Tyne estuary in the years after the Tynemouth tramcar system had been abandoned in 1921. (D. R. Harvey Collection)

11 (FT 1386) (Opposite below)
A slight bit of trouble! The SOS S single-deckers were very reliable, though they had to be started by hand with the starting handle. The four-cylinder side-valve 4.344 litre petrol engine had cylinder heads modified by the Ricardo Company. Harry Ricardo, the engineering genius who had set up the company, realised that turbulence within the combustion chamber increased flame speed. He developed the induction swirl chamber in the cylinders, a design that embodied a reasonable rate of pressure rise and good fuel consumption. The result was that from the SOS engine a remarkable economy and performance was possible, though the engine was less easy to start than some other contemporary petrol engines, as shown here. The use of the word Tynemouth on the radiator header tank is noteworthy. (D. R. Harvey Collection)

Potteries Motor Traction

61 (EH 6007) (Below)

One of the earliest of PMT's 1925 batch of SOS S models was 62 (EH 6007). This was SOS chassis number 29. Bodied by Brush with a B31F body, 61, one of a batch of the thirty-one S types delivered to PMT, was a surprisingly long-lived single-decker, surviving in service until 1935. Standing in front of the Potteries-embossed radiator filler cap is Driver Harold Forrester, wearing the sort of bus driver's uniform that, with its leather boots, epaulettes, metal buttons and cap, would not have looked that much out of place on a Great War battlefield. (J. Cooke Collection)

55 (EH 5148) (Opposite above)

This is the one exception. This early SOS S type built by BMMO on a TSM TS3 chassis frame and fitted with an orthodox clutch and gearbox was numbered 35 (EH 5148) in the PMT fleet. It was bodied by Davidson, who was a coach-builder based on the Trafford Park Industrial Estate in Manchester, with a thirty-one-seat charabanc body. The company supplied a total of eighteen charabanc bodies on S type chassis with a capacity of thirty-two seats, of which just one, 35, was delivered to Potteries in 1924. Strictly speaking the body was not a charabanc as it did not have doors for each row of seats and was known as the 'Corridor Coach' with a centre gangway. On a hot day in Matlock in the year of its delivery, this SOS S coach is weighed down with a total of thirty-six passengers, including a babe-in-arms and three children plus the driver. Even allowing for the children, the vehicle was definitely overladen. (J. Cooke Collection)

81 (EH 7101) (Right)
A line-up of seven S types led by 81 (EH 7101) await their next duty when parked in the newly opened Stoke-on-Trent garage. This bus was one of the last six SOS S types, numbered 81–86, that entered service in 1925, and all remained in service for ten years in largely this condition, which was a remarkable tribute to their original design. The six-bay, thirty-one-seater Brush-built body on 81 shows the steep entry steps, a far cry from today's front entrance, single-step single-deckers! (J. Cooke Collection)

82 (EH 7102) (Above)
Apparently standing in Hartshill when still fairly new is 82 (EH 7102). PMT purchased forty-three SOS S types and 82 was one of the last batch of six which entered service in late 1925 and were the last S types supplied to the operator, as 88–89 were the new forward-control FS types. 82 had the usual BET-styled Brush body, which was not only being supplied to Midland Red and the associated operators who were buying BMMO chassis but also to operators such as Thames Valley and East Kent, although other bodies of a similar design were built by Strachan & Brown and Ransomes. (R. Marshall Collection)

Trent Motor Traction
919 (CH 5430) (Opposite top)
A brand-new Trent SOS S single-decker, CH 5430 was one of thirty purchased by Trent Motor Traction in 1926. Unusually, they had Ransomes B31F bodies. It was renumbered 701 in 1930 after being rebuilt and lowered, which converted it to SOS ODD type. Twenty-one S types were converted to ODDs when they were all rebodied by United with a stylish B26F body. In this form, the transformed CH 5430 was eventually withdrawn in 1936. (D. R. Harvey Collection)

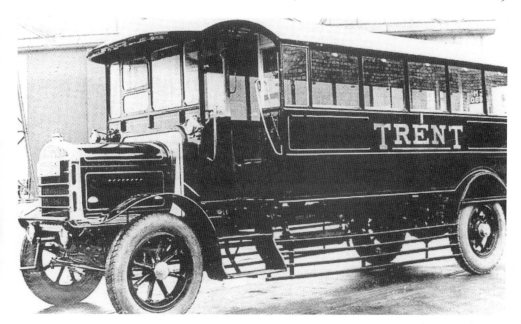

927 (CH 5448) (Above)

Standing in front of Alfreton garage is a virtually new SOS S 927 (CH 5448). This can be deduced from the unpainted bulkhead panel behind the bonnet and below the two-piece windscreen. This was the clue that this S type had a body from an earlier vehicle, in this case a Ransomes B31F body from an 809 1922 Daimler CM chassis. These Ransomes bodies were considerably lower when fitted to the Daimler chassis and were less influenced by Mr Wyndham Shire's dictates on the design of SOS bodies. 927 is waiting to work on the 21 service from Alfreton to Mansfield. The garage in Gooker Lane was opened in 1926, not long before this photograph was taken. The garage was used right through to the National Bus Company days, well into the mid-1970s. (R. Marshall Collection)

Ortona, Cambridge

36 (ER 3143) (Above)

Standing in Cambridge town centre when working on the service to Newmarket is Ortona's 36 (ER 3143). This SOS S type single-decker normal-control bus had the BMMO chassis number 7 and, although fitted with the cast name Ortona on the radiator header tank, would undoubtedly have been built using numerous chassis components from Tilling-Stevens. The bus was taken over by the fledgling Eastern Counties Company in 1931, becoming their S36, and it survived until 1937. (D. R. Harvey Collection)

45 (ER 5302) (Opposite top)

The Ransomes body on Ortona's SOS S type is well loaded on the Hallack & Bond's works outing with noticeably only one exception, the ladies sitting inside the bus and the gentlemen and the driver standing outside. They were high-class grocers who were based in Market Hill. The bus is ER 5302, which was built in 1926 and was numbered 26 in the Cambridge company's fleet, having entered service in March of that year. This bus was rebuilt in 1930 as an SOS ODD type and fitted with a United B26F body. In this form it was transferred to the newly formed Eastern Counties Omnibus Company on 14 July 1931, surviving until 1937. (The Cambridgeshire Collection)

Peterborough Electric

S3 (FL 3951) (Above)

The Peterborough Electric fleet of the 1920s consisted of mainly forty-eight-seat Leyland LB5s, such as FL 4217 to the rear, while standardising on SOS S type single-deckers. The leading bus is S3 (FL 3951), which was an SOS conversion of a Tilling-Stevens TS3 chassis and was fitted with a Ransomes, Simms and Jefferies twenty-eight-seater body. RSJ were based in Ipswich and bodied some fifty-five SOS S types of which this company had six, including S3. The bus is working on the service to the Great Northern Railway Station. (W. Noel Jackson Collection)

S14 (FL 4756) (Above)
The Fenland town of Whittlesey is located six miles from the city of Peterborough. In this photograph, Sid Harrimaway, the conductor who hailed from Whittlesey, is seen standing alongside the bus. The Buttercross dates back to 1680, but fell into disrepair in the nineteenth century and was about to be demolished when a local businessman donated some slate tiles for the roof. By the 1920s it served as a bus shelter. Peterborough Electric's S14 (FL 4756) stands alongside the ancient Buttercross in the town's market place. This Ransomes-bodied twenty-eight-seater entered service in November 1925 and remained in service until 1937. (D. R. Harvey Collection)

S18 (FL 4760) (Opposite top)
Being given a check-over in the Peterborough Electric garage with the bonnet having been taken off is S18 (FL 4760). This revealed the free-revving four-cylinder side-valve SOS-designed 4.344 litre petrol engine fitted with Ricardo combustion chambers in the modified cylinder heads, which produced the kind of performance which when in competition with electric tramcars would 'leave them for dead'! Although the SOS S type was considered to be operationally quite a small bus, with only twenty-eight seats, when compared to the two gentlemen working on the bus it can be seen that these single-deckers were actually surprisingly large. (D. R. Harvey Collection)

Llandudno Royal Blue

CC 4816 (Above)

CC4816 was one of the Tilling-Stevens TS3s fabricated by BMMO with crash gearboxes which actually pre-dated the genuine SOS S types. Although virtually identical to the S types, these buses still retained their TSM chassis numbers, which in this case was 4030. Llandudno Royal Blue CC 4816 was fitted with a Brush B32F body and survived long enough to become 504 in the Crosville fleet after the takeover in 1931. It was one of ten S types supplied new to the company but was one of only four that survived in this condition, as the remainder were converted to ODD type and given new Short B26F bodies. (D. R. Harvey Collection)

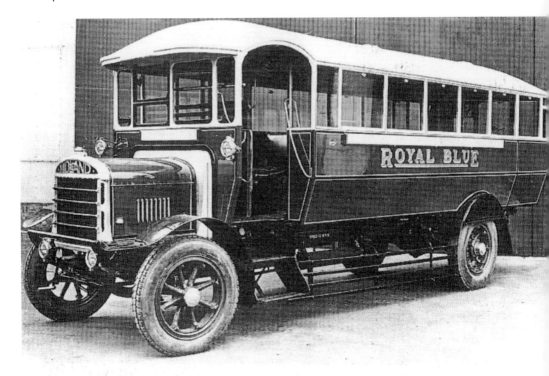

CC *6121*

The Llandudno Royal Blue Company received four SOS S types in 1924, two in 1925, four in 1926 and the final pair of S types built by BMMO in 1927. Although on the chassis frame the maximum speed of these thirty-two-seaters was shown as 12 mph, these normal-control single-deckers were capable of well in excess of 30 mph. This is CC 6121, which was one of the quartet built in 1926, and is seen prior to delivery at Carlyle Road Works. Noticeable are the artillery wheels, the lack of front-wheel braking and the single rear wheels. This style of lightweight body on the SOS S chassis was also produced by Brush of Loughborough and Ransomes, Simms & Jefferies of Ipswich, although the Royal Blue ones were constructed at Carlyle Road Works. (D. R. Harvey Collection)

SOS FS Type (Forward Steering)

In 1925 the first forward-control single-decker was developed. This was the FS model with thirty-four seats. Mechanically it was the same as the S type with the four-cylinder side-valve 4.344 litre petrol engine and a four-speed gearbox. In its bus form the FS weighed 4 tons 2 cwt, whereas the charabanc version was seven hundredweight less. Smaller diameter tyres enabled the FS type to be two inches lower. For the first time, the driver sat over the fuel tank which was mounted in the cab.

Despite eighty-seven FS vehicles being built, only two were sold, both of these going to Potteries Motor Traction in 1926.

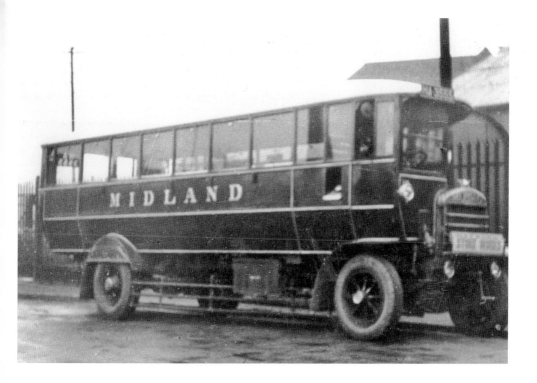

BMMO

608 (HA 3505)
One of the eighty-five FS buses delivered to Midland Red was HA 3505. Moving the driver to a position alongside the engine enabled these forward-control service buses to accommodate thirty-four passengers, which was two more than the previous S type. This Brush-bodied bus entered service in 1926 and although the body had an extra bay, the style, with its pronounced rocker panels and enormous ground clearance, was a direct development from the SOS S type. The Midland Red examples had the fuel tank beneath the driver's seat, which was a feature not found on the PMT pair. HA 3505, when still quite new, is parked in Bromsgrove, possibly at the town's railway station and is working on the route to Stoke Works. (J. Brown)

Potteries Motor Traction

88 (EH 7901)

Only two SOS FS single-deckers were sold by BMMO to any other operator and both of them went to Potteries Motor Traction in 1926. They were both fitted with Brush B34F bodies and lasted until 1935. The single-deck bogie Potteries Electric Traction tramcar is car 82. This forty-seater had been built by Midland RCW in 1900 and mounted on Mountain & Gibson Brill type 22E bogies, which had recently been rebuilt with new 40 hp GE249A motors and which would be sold to Wemyss District in 1928. The bus and the tram are standing near May Bank depot in Wolstanton. It was these early SOS buses which literally killed off so many tramway systems, especially in the Black Country, while the PET 4-foot 0-inch gauge tramway was rapidly brought to an end on 11 July 1928 when the successors to these SOS FSs, some fifty QL types, were introduced earlier the same year. So this pair of FS buses was the precursor to the buses which closed the Potteries system. (D. R. Harvey Collection)

SOS Q (Queen)

The SOS Q developed because of BMMO's desire to increase the seating capacity of their standard single-decker from thirty-four to thirty-seven seats. The wheelbase was extended by a foot to 16 feet and 7½ inches. This increase in the wheelbase length enabled the body to be fitted with an extra seventh bay, while the length of the cab was dramatically reduced by moving the bulkhead as far forward as possible. Thus the prototype vehicle was a long-wheelbase FS but with the exception of the prototype, HA 3532, all the other buses had the engine offset to the nearside, which enabled the cab-space for the driver to be slightly wider. The offset radiator introduced on this model was to become a standard feature on all subsequent pre-war SOS models. These were the last SOS buses to only have rear-wheel brakes. The Midland Red examples weighed 4 tons 4.5 cwt. The Q was 26 feet 6 inches long, 7 feet 2.75 inches wide and 9 feet 5 inches high. This was the only SOS Q built in 1926 and this prototype was delivered to Midland Red. The following year BMMO had a further 109 Qs, but seven other operators purchased another ninety-one of the model.

BMMO
686 (HA 3602)
The arrival of Midland Red in the Leicester area began as early as 1922 with services operating to Coalville, Coventry and Nuneaton. The third Midland Red garage to open in the city was located over Roman remains in Southgate Street, with accommodation for ninety buses. The garage was opened on 21 July 1927, just three days after this photograph was taken. HA 3602 was one of thirty-five SOS Qs delivered to Midland Red in that year and was built with a Carlyle-built B37F body. The Q was longer than the previous FS model, with a larger overhang behind the rear axle. This gave the Q model a seating capacity which was three more than the model it succeeded. It was also noticeably lower, which improved access for intending passengers and modernised the appearance of these buses, although the vertical windscreen really didn't help. HA 3602 survived until 1936. (J. Cooper Collection)

674 (HA 3600) (Above)
Within two years of the introduction of the SOS Q type, low-framed single-deckers such as
the Leyland 'Tiger' TS1, 2 and 3s, AEC 'Regal' 662 and the Bristol B had all been put into
production and immediately made the Carlyle Road Works products look old-fashioned.
Still looking more or less in 'as-built' condition with peculiar half-moon rear mudguards,
cycle-type front wing and a high chassis level revealing the exhaust pipe and silencer, HA
3600 stands in Grantham Bus Station in August 1933. Despite its vintage appearance, this
bus has another three years work in front of it. (G. H. F. Atkins, courtesy J. Banks)

Northern General
318 (CN 2867) (Opposite above)
The SOS 'Queen' 318, (CN 2867), shows just how short the driver's cab and engine
compartment was. 318 is brand new in April 1927 and reveals that the passenger-carrying
part of the single-decker, built by Brush, was very much intended for the carrying of
passengers. The Q body had a capacity of thirty-seven and had the advantage over the earlier
S types by having three shallower steps up into the saloon. This very early development of
SOS buses shows that the body still retains the Gothic porch entrance and a spare wheel
carried in the long overhang behind the rear axle. (Courtesy Go Ahead Northern)

309 (CN 2858) (Opposite below)
Northern General received all of their twenty-five SOS Qs in 1927. 309 (CN 2858) entered
service in March 1927 and was fitted with a Brush B37F body. During the 1930s the
original angular side-panelling and rocker panels were replaced with curved lower panels
which considerably modernised the appearance of these Brush bodies. 309 survived until
1946 while the SOS S HA 2440, new in 1925 and rebodied with a Short B36F body in
1933, survived until 1952. (D. R. Harvey Collection)

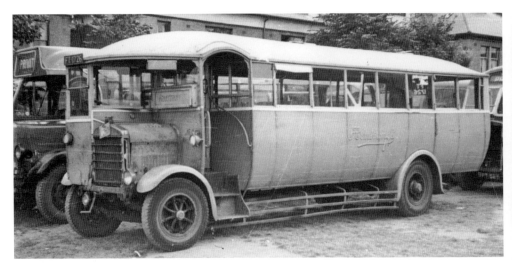

Tynemouth

20 (FT 1726) (Opposite above)

There were eleven SOS Qs delivered to Tynemouth and District in 1927 which were numbered 12, 14–23, (FT 1556–1561, 1725–1727 and 1749–1750). There was reputedly no fleet number 13, though 12 was sometimes quoted as being numbered 13! All eleven were fitted with the standard style of Brush B37F body which, despite this company's ties with Northern General, were ordered as a discrete batch to those contemporary Qs being delivered to the parent operator, as the BMMO body numbers were in a later batch. 20 (FT 1726) is in surprisingly original condition save for the saloon side-panelling, which has been modernised by eliminating the rocker panelling. This modification appears to have been undertaken on many of these early forward-control SOS Qs owned by the Northern Group. 20 was one of nine of the batch that was transferred to Northern General in 1927, but was the only one sold for further service. Here it is parked and flanked by Leyland 'Tiger' TS7 models operated by United and Sunderland District when being operated by Armstrong of Ebchester, near Consett as their number 4 in the late 1940s. (D. R. Harvey Collection)

Potteries

98 (EH 9801) (Opposite middle)

Only eleven SOS Qs were delivered to Potteries Motor Traction and all were fitted with standard Brush B37F bodies. They were numbered 92–101 with registrations EH 9011–9016 and EH 9801–9804. When working on a private hire in about 1930 are 98 on the left and 99. The two buses each had a seating capacity of thirty-seven but it would appear that it is going to be something of a squeeze as there are approximately seventy-eight people on this private hire. It is indicative of the social mores of the time that only ten of the men are bareheaded, with the remainder wearing either trilby hats or caps, while all of the women are wearing hats. (J. Cooke Collection)

Trent

958 (CH 6239) (Opposite below)

Parked in Huntingdon Street Bus Station in Nottingham is one of Trent Motor Traction's twenty-five SOS Qs delivered in 1927. The spoked front wheels on 958 (CH 6239) reveal that the SOS Q model was not equipped with front brakes, with the driver having to rely on the footbrake only operating on the single-tyred rear axle. Modernised with curved side-panels in 1933, 958 is beautifully painted in its red-and-brown lined-out livery, which somehow seems to emphasise the tiny cab area and the long passenger compartment. This bus was withdrawn in 1938, having achieved some eleven years of service and eventually ended its days with a Birmingham-based showman named Smith. (W. J. Haynes)

970 (CH 6251) (Top)
Delivered in 1927, this SOS Q, built for Trent Motor Traction as their 970 (CH 6251),
waits in Derby's Art Deco Bus Station soon after its opening in 1933. It is about to leave on
the service to Alfreton. This was the first purpose-built bus station in the United Kingdom
and was designed by Charles Herbert Aslin, the Derby Borough Architect. It was the first
of its kind in the world, with railway-style platforms. This famous, iconic bus station
closed in October 2005 and was demolished in July 2006. Behind 970 stands the two-
years-younger SOS M 407 (CH 8115). The beautiful finish on both buses disguises their
somewhat old-fashioned appearance, while the M type's lower build and fitment of four-
wheel brakes makes the Q type seem quite antiquated. (D. R. Harvey Collection)

955 (CH 6233) (Opposite below)

Seen as a caravan owned by a Derby-based showman named Eaton, CH 6233 is at a fair at Stockport in March 1950. This former Trent Motor Traction single-decker bus, an SOS Q, had been numbered 955. Looking remarkably complete, despite being sold in 1938 and surviving through the Second World War, a number of the windows had been panelled over and the remaining four had been rebuilt with more substantial frames. The box on the roof would have been used to store fairground equipment and covered with a tarpaulin when the fairground moved sites. (C. Wright/PM Photography)

Llandudno Royal Blue (No photograph)

There were five SOS Qs delivered to Llandudno Royal Blue in 1927. They were registered CC6821–6825 and were fitted with Brush B37F. After the company was taken over by Crosville in 1931, the buses were numbered 512–516 and lasted until 1933 before being withdrawn.

Ortona, Cambridge

55 (ER 7105) (Below)

The Ortona Motor Co. started operation on 1 August 1907 through a Mr James Walford, who renamed the defunct Cambridge Motor Bus Co. after a seaside town in Italy that he had passed whilst on a recent cruise. The early Ortona bus fleet standardised on Straker-Squire chassis but by 1925 the single-decker of choice was to be manufactured by BMMO. The second generation of Ortona SOS types were the fast, lightweight Q types. Waiting in Cambridge Bus Station when working on the Cambridge to Saffron Walden service is the first of the Ortona's seven SOS thirty-seven-seater Qs, 55 (ER 7105). Delivered between March and May 1927, all seven were reseated to B36F in 1937 and were withdrawn and converted to ambulances in September 1939 on the outbreak of the Second World War. (W. Noel Jackson Collection)

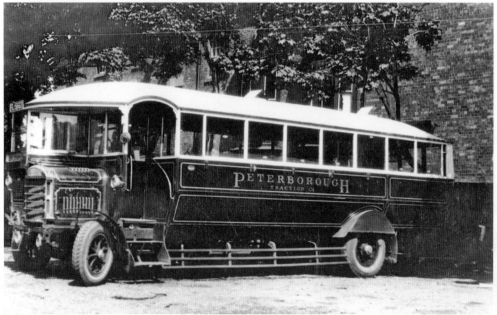

54 (ER 7107) (Top)

The SOS Q was an upgraded forward-control version of the S and the passenger section of the body, in this case built by Brush, was distinctly an extended S type design. Where it did differ was in the front of the vehicle where the driver's cab was brought forward alongside the short in length but rather tall engine compartment. The driver sat over the petrol tank in a cab, which at the rear was of adequate width but at the front was extremely narrow. Ortona's 54 (ER 7107) was brand-new when it was posed for an official photograph in 1927 before it entered service and lacking the side destination slip boards. (The Cambridgeshire Collection)

Peterborough Electric

Q1 (FL 5663) (Opposite below)

The Peterborough Electric Traction's trams were finally abandoned on 15 November 1930 after twenty-seven years of operation, though except for a ghost tram running on every route, no passengers had been carried since 4 August 1930. Standing beneath the trees in central Peterborough on a warm summer's day is a Brush-bodied SOS Q Q1 (FL 5663). This Brush-bodied thirty-seven-seater entered service in March 1927 and so was well over two years old by the time the open-top trams were replaced, though both the trams and the Qs looked obsolete. The noticeable feature of these early SOS buses was just how high the steps were in order to gain access into the saloon through the Gothic arch porch. (W. J. Haynes)

Q2 (FL 5664) (Below)

This was one of eight SOS Qs supplied to Peterborough Electric in 1927 and Q2 (FL 5664) stands alongside the tram tracks on the eastern side of the Market Place in Peterborough City Centre. To the far left is the edge of *The Bird in Hand* public house. Behind the bus is the 'Lounge Café' of Mr A. H. Gibson; next-door is the butcher's shop of Mr F. W. Brown, with the words 'Market Place' either side of the single-bay window while to the far right is the edge of the jewellers shop of Mr G. R. Noakes. The deep-roofed, Brush-bodied thirty-seven-seat single-decker is in its original condition with angular two-piece rocker panels and its single rear wheels partially covered by half-moon-shaped mudguards. The canvas flap in the driver's door window is there in order to expedite hand signals in inclement weather. (Southdown Enthusiasts Club)

Q8 (FL 6466) (Above)
Parked inside the old tram depot in Lincoln Road, Millfield, Peterborough, is Q8
(FL 6466), the second bus in the line. It is in company with the outside-staircase,
highbridge Hall Lewis-bodied Leyland 'Titan' TD1 and a pair of lowbridge Leyland-
bodied TD1s. The single-decker on the extreme left is one of the twelve SOS Ms of 1929,
which were considerably lower that the older Q in front of it. The angular lines of the Q's
Brush body belonged to a BET style developed in the mid-1920s that was also found on
Tilling-Stevens B9 and B10 chassis for a number of other operators, though it has more
in common with the body style of the double-decker in front of it than the stylish Leyland
bodies at the front of the line. (D. R. Harvey Collection)

SOS QC (Queen Charabanc)

In 1927 and 1928, BMMO produced a normal-control, thirty-seat, canvas-roofed coach
based on the running units of the Q bus. Unlike the true charabanc these buses had a
single entrance, which was positioned towards the front of the saloon. These touring
coaches had a central gangway with seven rows of seats in the body of the coach and a
pair of seats in front of the entrance door alongside the driver, who sat behind a heavily
raked steering wheel. There were side windows that could be lowered and the rear dome
was fixed. The roll-top canvas roof could be lowered and raised in minutes according to
the publicity of the time. The engine was centrally mounted and as a result the front of
the bus had a less lopsided look than the SOS Q bus.
    Midland Red had the bulk of the constructed coaches, having fourteen, and the only
other operator to receive the QC was Trent, who purchased five.

BMMO

667 (HA 3666) (Right)

The SOS QC touring coaches, with their deeply upholstered seven pairs of two seats, were not charabancs as they did not have individual doors for each row of seats. HA 3666 had its canvas roof rolled back into the fixed rear dome and it was attached to the runners above the fixed side windows. The

long normal-control bonnet was an impressive feature of these coaches although it must have made the driver's view of the road somewhat limited; this was not helped by the high, strangely angled steering wheel. Nevertheless, it was still a very impressive-looking vehicle! (Midland Red)

Trent Motor Traction

603 (CH 6259) (Below)

The five Trent Motor Traction SOS QLs were built in 1927 and received Carlyle Works thirty-seat open touring coach bodies. These canvas-roof normal-control-bodied coaches were virtually identical to the fourteen that went to Midland Red. The five Trent QCs were given fleet numbers 600–604 and registered CH6256–6260. On the QL the front wheels, lacking brakes, were smaller than those on the rear axle and as a result this somewhat emphasised the depth of the large bonnet. Here 603 (CH 6259) stands outside the luxurious Clarendon Hotel in Cornmarket in Oxford's city centre. The Clarendon was an ancient coaching inn, known as the Star for at least 400 years until renamed in 1863 and survived at 52 Cornmarket until it was closed in 1954. (D. R. Harvey Collection)

SOS QL (Queen Low)

The SOS QL was a further evolution of the forward-control SOS chassis. It was mechanically the same as the Q chassis of 1927 but they were the first chassis to come out of Carlyle Road Works to be fitted with four-wheel brakes. The bus was just a quarter of an inch shorter at 26 feet 5.75 inches long, but with the introduction of twin rear wheels, the overall height went down by two inches to 9 feet 3 inches. The result was that the side skirt panels were deeper, which gave the impression of being lower than it actually was. The multi-windowed lightweight body still retained the eight-bay construction of the previous SOS Q and weighed 4 tons 8 cwt 1 qtr.

The QL was only in production during 1928 and this was BMMO's most successful model, with many of the buses for both Midland Red and the operators to which they were sold lasting into the late 1940s. In all BMMO built a record total of 381 vehicles in 1928 but the most successful of all was the QL type. Midland Red took 170 QLs, while another 179 were sold to six other operators.

BMMO

796 (HA 3726) (Opposite above)
Posed with its driver and conductor with his Bell Punch ticket machine and some passengers in the centre of Swadlincote in about 1934 is the beautifully lined-out HA 3726. This SOS QL had a Brush B37F body and had a distinct advantage over previous SOS models in that it had brakes fitted to the front axle. Thus the front wheels were discs rather than being open-spoked. The lower build of these buses is notable due to the dropped chassis frame rather than the height of the body. This batch of QLs included the fifty Potteries buses of 1928. The slip board on the bulkhead shows the bus is going to Burton via Stanton. 796 had a ten-year service life, although some of the later buses managed to survive another ten years. (D. R. Harvey Collection)

902 (HA 4841) (Opposite below)
In 1944 Midland Red, who had not used fleet numbers on their buses, began to use their A numbers, which had been only used as private identification numbers as an office paper record, as fleet numbers. The sixth-oldest bus to carry the new fleet number was a venerable SOS QL dating from 1928 and was part of the same batch that were delivered directly to Peterborough Electric. HA 4841, with a Ransomes body, received the fleet number 902 and had been reseated in 1935 to B35F with ON type seats. Throughout the Second World War it had been converted to an ambulance. As it therefore had quite a low mileage, it survived in service until 1949. 902 is parked in the waste ground in front of Digbeth garage in about 1947, with the Birmingham City Transport tram lines visible alongside the parked Austin Eight. (D. R. Harvey Collection)

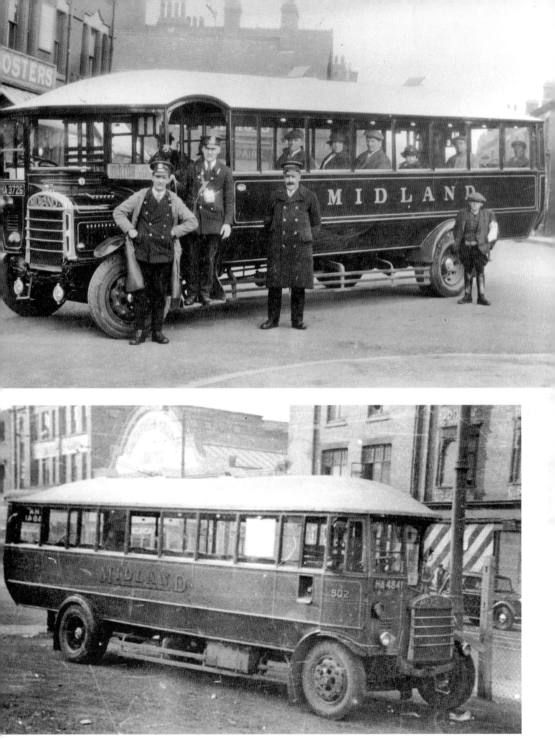

Northern General

347 (UP 560) (Above)

Standing alongside 368 (UP 680), an SOS QLC normal-control touring coach, is another brand-new Midland Red-built SOS bus. This is 347 (UP 560), a Brush thirty-seven-seater QL. Both vehicles were built in 1928, but the Brush-bodied QL, despite its antiquated appearance, does look forward towards the future development of the single-decker service bus whereas the touring coach, with its driver sitting with the passengers behind the engine and having a fully opening canvas roof, was effectively one of the last throws of the dice in the charabanc/touring coach design. Both vehicles are parked, awaiting customers for the possible hire. (Courtesy Go Ahead Northern)

424 (BR 6765) (Opposite above)

Share's furniture store was based in Fawcett Street, one of the main shopping thoroughfares in the centre of Sunderland. This apparent link with Wearside is continued by the BR-registered Northern General Brush-bodied SOS QL. 424 (BR 6765) was one of ten Brush-bodied, Sunderland-registered SOS QLs and this bus entered service in October 1928 and survived until the very end of QL operation in January 1950. This 1930s view of the bus shows that it had been used on a school's special, though the use of the word SCHOLARS is redolent of the Geordie vernacular. The deep, bright red bus livery is beautifully lined out in gold and black, displaying the company's corporate pride in its buses. (Courtesy Go Ahead Northern)

391 (CN 3686) (Opposite below)

Northern General's 391 (CN 3686) was one of just fourteen SOS QLs bodied by Ransomes, Sims & Jefferies. These, like the Brush-bodied QLs, also had a B37F layout. The bus has its bonnet open, revealing the very compact four-cylinder side-valve 4.344 litre petrol engine. As with earlier SOS buses, the four-speed gearbox was an advantage, giving the vehicles the speedy capability that enabled them to compete with trams as well as small, slow, 'village' buses. 391 stands in Stanley garage yard on 25 March 1950, sometime after withdrawal, having already lost its outer rear wheels. (D. F. Tee)

UP 572 (Opposite above)
Tynemouth and District bought five SOS QL buses through their parent Northern General Company in 1928 and these were identical to the NGT vehicles. They were numbered 24–27 (FT 1777–1780) and 34 (FT 1884) while in 1929 UP 555–556 were allocated numbers 35–36 in the Tynemouth & District fleet. (W. J. Haynes)

UP551 (Opposite middle)
After years languishing away, the SOS QL was finally completed in the spring of 2012. Northern General's 338 (UP551) was the 600th chassis built at Carlyle Road and had entered service in March 1928, being the first of sixty-five QLs supplied to the company. It was fitted with a Brush thirty-seven-seat body which was divided by a partition halfway along the saloon with a front non-smokers compartment. This framework also served to strengthen the somewhat lightweight body construction. Although fitted with a large destination box, 338 remained largely in its original condition, latterly from Consett garage, until it was withdrawn at the beginning of 1950 as one of the final nine NGT QLs. After that it was used for some time as a caravan at Bardon Mill, a village in the River South Tyne valley on the main A69 road between Newcastle-upon-Tyne and Carlisle. 338 was rescued for spares in 1965 by Robert Atkinson and was moved to Beamish Open Air Museum in 1978, when the restoration was started by the Friends of Beamish Museum, who have constructed a new body identical to the original Brush design of 1928. It is seen parked in the main street of the museum in 2012. (D. R. Harvey)

Potteries Motor Traction
107 (VT 806) (Opposite above)
Potteries Motor Traction purchased exactly fifty SOS QL chassis and all of these vehicles, which entered service in 1928, received Brush B37 bodies. Despite being a service bus, 107 (VT 806) is being used on a day excursion to Blackpool and stands alongside the old big dipper on the Pleasure Beach. Unlike QLs in other fleets, the PMT ones had comparatively short lives as they were withdrawn between 1935 and 1939, with this bus going in 1936 and then being sold to a showman, a fate which befell many of PMT's SOS-built vehicles. 107 is parked behind VT 1538, which appears to be a Leyland-bodied Leyland 'Lion' PLSC3. (N. Hamshere)

118 (VT 817) (Left)

A close-up of the front of PMT's 118 (VT 817) reveals just how antiquated these buses actually were! It also shows just how dangerous ordinary glass could be before the days of safety glass, as the broken windscreen's shards of glass look distinctly unhealthy! Some of the details on this PMT SOS QL are worthy of comment, including the pair of low-mounted headlights and the huge side-lights. The cab itself, as on all of these early forward-control SOS types, looks as though it has been built on as an afterthought. The engine bay did not intrude into the structure, making the QLs look even more like a normal-control S type with a cab on the side. 118 was another PMT withdrawal of 1936. (J. Cooke Collection)

150 (VT 849) (Below)

The nearside of 150 (VT 849) shows that the SOS QL model was very much of a transitional model. The high floor-line and steep entrance steps were somehow masked by the long, almost sleek 26-foot 5.75-inch bodywork. The short length of the engine and bonnet somehow conceals just how narrow the driver's cab was. Seen parked at Alton, the PMT QLs were quickly fitted with a rather ungainly front canopy-mounted destination box. These Brush-bodied examples could be easily distinguished from the Ransomes-bodied QLs by having a very simple and small angled section linking the front bulkhead just forward of the Gothic-arched porch entrance to the canopy roof. (D. R. Harvey Collection)

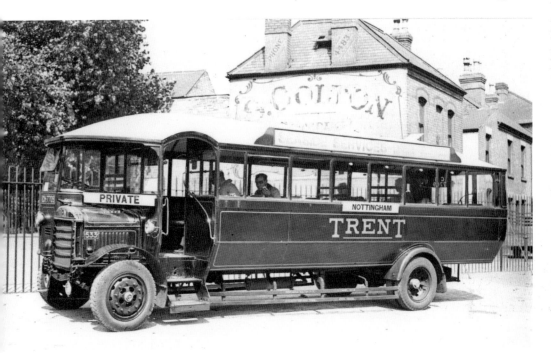

Trent

533 (CH 7709)

Trent Motor Traction purchased thirty-eight SOS QL chassis in 1928, of which sixteen were bodied by Ransomes with the usual B37F layout. There was hardly any difference between these bodies and those supplied by Brush, though the small canopy bracket was more substantial on the Ransomes bodies. Each had seven and a half-bay construction bodies with a bulkhead halfway down the body which also served to separate non-smokers at the front from smokers to the rear. These were the last BMMO single-deck buses to have this intermediate bulkhead. The QLs were also the last to be fitted with cycle-style front wings. 533 (CH 7709) stands in Huntingdon Street bus station, Nottingham in September 1933 with its crew taking a well-earned break. (G. H. F. Atkins, courtesy J. Banks)

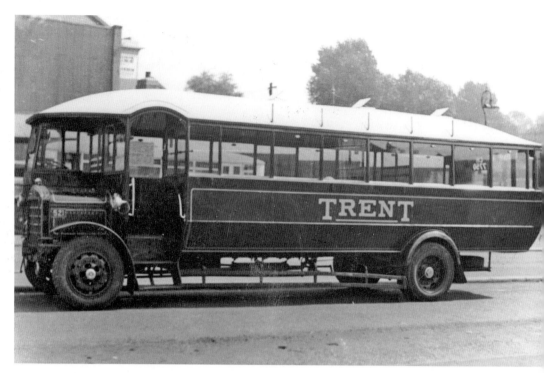

521 (CH 7750) (Opposite above)
The Brush-bodied QLs could also be distinguished from those bodied by Ransomes by the slightly different narrow windows at the rear of the saloon. 521 (CH 7750) entered service in October 1928 and is seen parked in Huntingdon Street Bus Station in Nottingham about five years later. The Trent QLs were not as long-lived as the earlier Qs, being withdrawn during 1937, but this one went to Northern General as their 839 where it survived as a bus until 1941, whereupon it was converted into an ambulance. Parts of this bus survive in the preserved NGT SOS QL UP 551. (W. J. Haynes)

838 (CH 7749) (Opposite below)
CH 7749 is seen as Northern General's 838; it was originally Trent Motor Traction's 531 and entered service in October 1928. It was purchased by Northern General, along with five other former Trent QLs, in 1938 and was given the fleet number 838. The NGT Group rather favoured these late 1920s SOS chassis types and by transferring them, dramatically increased the longevity of these six buses, with 838 lasting in service until 1950. (D. R. Harvey Collection)

Peterborough Electric
QL4 (FL 7370) (Above)
Peterborough Electric bought five SOS QLs in 1928 and when taken over by Eastern Counties in 1931. QL4 entered service in December 1928 and survived in service until 1938. It went through the Ministry of Supply to the Home Timber Production Department in Bristol and survived only until the end of 1942. The appearance of the Peterborough Electric SOS was dramatically altered when they were acquired by the Eastern Counties Company. Fitted with huge Bible board destination blinds, flimsily held in position by two thin iron rods and lit externally from both sides, in this condition they looked almost as though they might pitch forward under the strain of such a structure! This hot, sunny day helps to show off that nearly all the side windows could be opened and that they were of the full drop type. (J. Smith/Lens of Sutton)

Llandudno Royal Blue

CC 7744 (Above)

Standing outside the garage at Pen-y-Gwryd near Beddgelert is Llandudno Royal Blue's CC 7744. The operation of these QLs by the Llandudno-based company was unusual in that these small-engined, lightweight capacity buses with fairly high seating capacities for the time, tended to be purchased by operators with less arduous terrains. After a stiff climb into Snowdonia from Caernarvon and then having to face going down again to Llandudno via Capel Curig and Betws-y-Coed, the driver is filling up the radiator of the bus as a precaution before continuing his journey. Later to be numbered 520 in the Crosville fleet, this SOS QL had a Brush B37F body and entered service in 1928 in the attractive blue livery of the company that suited these buses so well. (Courtesy H. Peers)

CC 7748 (Opposite top)

By the end of 1930 Crosville Motor Services had control of most of the services in north and central Wales – as well as in the neighbouring English county of Cheshire and on the Wirral peninsula – and were well on the way to buying out competing operators. This was the case with Llandudno Royal Blue, whose sixteen of SOS QLs buses were all transferred to Crosville in February 1931 but due to being non-standard were sold after only three years service to PMT. In this brief interregnum, the buses were repainted in the full Crosville livery of maroon and had a fleet name which could hardly be misread! The driver of 524 (CC 7748) casually leans against his charge in the bright summer sunshine, which helps to illuminate the matchboard wooden interior saloon ceiling. (J. Nickels, via J. Carroll)

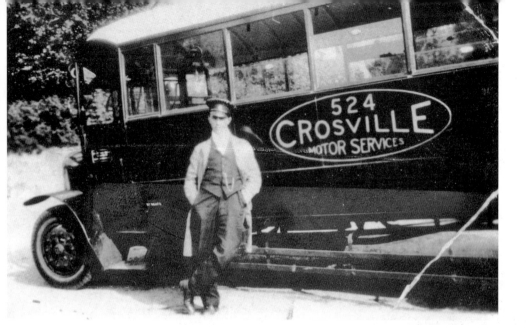

CC 7745 (Above)

CC 7745 was new in 1928 to Llandudno Coaching & Carriage Co., trading as Royal Blue, and sold out to the Crosville Company in February 1931. It was painted into Crosville's then maroon-and-cream livery and given the fleet number 521. By 1934, all of these QLs had been sold via a dealer in Hanley to Potteries Motor Traction, whereupon this bus became their fleet number 42. This is why it has a 'POTTERIES'-inscribed radiator header tank. After acquisition, PMT managed to squeeze another three years service out of CC 7745. It was then used as a caravan in the Llangollen area before being acquired for long-term preservation at the Wythall Bus Museum. It is seen there on 4 April 1988 awaiting restoration. (D. R. Harvey)

SOS QLC (Queen Low Charabanc)

This was another development of the normal-control touring coach. At first sight it looked very similar to the previous QL model, but being based on the QL it has equal-sized wheels and four-wheel brakes. The lowered chassis enabled the height of the coach to be reduced by three inches to 8 feet 2 inches. In all, eighty-five QLC chassis were constructed and all were bodied by Short Brothers with twenty-nine-seater bodywork.

The QLC however was in reality two quite distinct models. These coaches were built between 1928 and 1930, but the 1928 batch of thirty coaches had the standard four-cylinder 4.332 litre petrol engine coupled to a four-speed gearbox and were classified QLC4. They weighed 4 tons 8 cwt. From the 1928 production Northern General bought ten, Trent Motor Traction had three, while Llandudno Blue bought two.

The 1929 and 1930 chassis were all fitted with the newly developed six-cylinder 5.047 litre petrol engine, which had been experimentally fitted to a few of the SOS QL buses. These QLC6s were fitted with an attractive and more modern style of radiator and the extra weight of the larger engine increased the weight to 4 tons 14 cwt. Of these bigger-engined coaches PMT bought two, Trent purchased a further three and Llandudno Blue another pair.

BMMO
807 (HA 4830) (Above)
Loaded up and raring to go from the forecourt of a public house is SOS QLC HA 4830. This touring coach had a Short Brothers C29F body and dated from 1928. These coaches had four-cylinder engines and could be distinguished from the six-cylinder version of 1930 by having a radiator with three horizontal bars across it. This radiator style could trace its origins back to the Tilling-Stevens TS3s of fifteen years earlier. The predominantly male contingent of passengers are nearly all wearing hats, which although the norm for

the 1930s would have bee useful as the canvas roof has been folded back. This coach, being identical to those purchased by Northern General, was sold to that company in 1935 where it became their 690, surviving until 1939. (D. R. Harvey Collection)

1178 (HA 5144) (Above)
The six-cylinder SOS QLCs of 1930 carried a modernised radiator which was only used on SOS types for about two years. Standing in Southgate Street Bus Station in Leicester is HA 5144, awaiting passengers for the 23-mile-long service to Nottingham. The coach has its canvas roof erected and with nine ribbed roof-hoops and well-secured studs above the side windows, the coach would have been well protected from inclement weather. One can only imagine travelling in one of these QLC coaches with its roof in this position must have been akin to either being in a large touring car or even a mobile tent! Withdrawn in 1938, HA 5144 was retained by Midland Red until 1943. (W. J. Haynes)

Northern General

368 (UP 681) (Above)

With its canvas roof and side screens erected in case of inclement weather, Northern General's 368 (UP 681) is clearly one of the later SOS QLC touring coaches, as its solid front wheels show that the vehicle has front-wheel brakes. Entering service in June in 1928, 368 had a Short twenty-nine-seater body which although not a charabanc, a French word defined as a 'carriage with wooden benches' distinguished by having an entrance door for each row of seats, its body does show a direct lineage from that early type of touring vehicle. It also looks very dated, running only until 1937 whereupon it was converted into fire engine! (D. R. Harvey Collection)

369 (UP 682) (Opposite top)

The SOS QLC coaches looked very impressive when they had their canvas roofs folded away, although they did have a somewhat bow-shaped look about them. Standing outside the Gateshead garage of Northern General is their 369 (UP 682), which looks as if it has returned after a hard day's work. The QLC had the advantage of front-wheel brakes and was capable of a good turn of speed on excursions to the coast. The rear dome was fixed and the canvas roof, as shown here, could be folded up, enabling the twenty-nine passengers to 'benefit' from the fresh air as they bowled along. 369 was transferred in 1933 to Wakefields Motors of Tynemouth, an NGT subsidiary, as their W59. (Courtesy Go Ahead Northern)

Potteries Motor Traction (No photograph)

There were just two SOS QLCs delivered to Potteries Motor Traction in 1930. They were registered numbered 222 and 223 with registrations VT 4522–4523 and were fitted with Short C29F bodies. They were renumbered 12 and 11 in 1934 and were rebodied with Burlingham C36F bodies in 1936 and survived in this state until 1947.

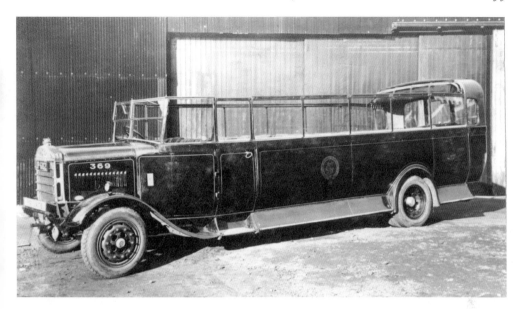

Trent Motor Traction

670 (CH 8919) (Above)

Waiting to load up in the Art Deco-styled Derby Bus Station before leaving on an excursion to Lathkill Dale in 1936 is Trent Motor Traction's 670 (CH 8919). This was one of the operator's three SOS QLC normal-control touring coaches, which were usually used on Peak District day excursions. These Trent examples were fitted with the plain radiator that was briefly used by BMMO in about 1930. Lathkill Dale is a limestone valley in the White Peak area of the Peak District National Park, which for many years was associated with mining for lead. Most of the lead had been exhausted by the eighteenth century but in the 1840s some of the deep mines were drained by steam-powered waterwheels. Today the drainage channels and spoil heaps look almost as if they are part of the natural landscape. (J. Cull)

Llandudno Royal Blue

CC 7862 (Above)

Posing in the Llanberis Pass with its canvas roof folded away into the permanent rear dome and loaded up with a full complement of twenty-nine passengers is CC 7862. This was the first of the pair delivered in 1928. Equipped with Short C29F bodies, these first two were fitted with the large 1920s-styled radiators. The date must be about 1929 as this period was epitomised by the style of ladies' cloche hats. This touring coach became 585 in the Crosville fleet. (J. Nickels, via J. Carroll)

CC 9285 (Opposite above)

The later SOS QLCs were built in 1930 with a more modern style of radiator, which to some extent masked the somewhat old-fashioned design of the normal-control touring coach. It was also a distinguishing feature between the earlier four-cylinder QLCs and these later six-cylinder vehicles. The radiator header tank carried the 'ROYAL' badge. CC9285, by now Crosville 588, is posed with its canvas roof folded back, exposing the twenty-nine seats. One advantage of the body design of these vehicles was that the side windows were fixed, which did prevent excessive draughts. (Ribble Enthusiasts Club)

CC 9284 (Opposite below)

With an ill-fitting canvas roof and looking distinctly careworn, CC 9284, by now numbered Q1 in the Crosville fleet, sits at the back of Sealand Road Works in Chester on 28 May 1949. At first glance it looks as if CC 9284 has been converted to a half-cab, but closer inspection reveals that it is parked alongside a withdrawn Leyland 'Cub'. In 1930, the QLC model was updated by the fitment of a six-cylinder 5.047 litre petrol engine. This meant that the bonnet was slightly longer and these later coaches were fitted with the more modern radiator. (D. R. Harvey Collection)

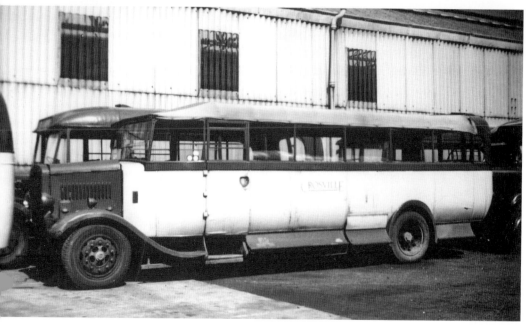

SOS ODD

By the end of the 1920s there was a rapidly developing need for a small bus suitable for less busy and/or rural services. The result was the SOS ODD type, which was rebuilt and modernised from the SOS S type. Fifty-one of the 1924 chassis were rebodied by United between 1929 and 1930 with attractive B26F bodywork. Although virtually the same length as the original S type on which they were based, they were 6.5 inches wider and at 9 feet 2.5 inches high were 4.5 inches lower. The prototype rebuild was HA 2393 and as a result of its success another fifty of these attractive buses were produced, with Trent Motor Traction, Llandudno Blue and Ortona receiving twenty-one, six and five respectively.

BMMO
494 (HA 2433) (Above)
Waiting sat the bus stop in St Owen Street, Hereford, outside the eleventh-century St Peter's Church is one of the very neat-looking SOS ODD single-deckers. HA 2433 originally entered service in 1925 with a B32F body constructed by Brush as an SOS S. The bus was one of forty-nine reconstructed in 1930 with new chassis frames and fitted with new United B26F bodywork. The result was very attractive, though the retention of the old-style radiator and the spoked front wheels, still without brakes, rather spoilt the whole effect. In this guise HA 2433 remained in service with Midland Red until 1938. (D. R. Harvey Collection)

Trent Motor Traction
916 (CH 5432) (Opposite top)
Trent MT's CH 5432 was originally fitted with a B31F body constructed by Ransomes when it entered service in 1926, but was one of those rebuilt as SOS ODD types in 1930. The chassis was lowered and fitted with a new, sleek-looking United B26F body but despite its much improved and more modern appearance, the ODDs still only had brakes on the rear axle. Originally numbered 916, after rebuilding the bus was renumbered 714. These little buses were ideal to open up new rural services which did not warrant a full-

sized thirty-four-seater. It is lying over on the parking area on Huntingdon Street Bus Station in Nottingham. (W. J. Haynes)

910 (CH 5428) (Above)
This is how many SOS types finished up! Seen at Rochester Bridge on 26 August 1951, the former Trent 910 (CH 5428) was a converted SOS ODD, although by this time the sleek lines of the United body had been considerably altered in order to be used as a showman's van. Towing a four-wheel drawbar trailer, from this angle CH 5428 reveals its ancestry by having single rear wheels. Somewhere in its more recent history, this stalwart of the fairground circuit has acquired a radiator with a 'MIDLAND'-inscribed header tank. (J. H. Meredith)

Ortona

39 (ER 5038)

Waiting in Drummer Street, Cambridge is SOS ODD 39 (ER 5038). The bus is about to leave on the service to Newmarket. In its original form ER 5038 was a thirty-seven-seater with a Brush body which entered service in February 1926. It only survived for four years in this form before being one of the five Ortona S types rebuilt with this attractively styled United B26F body as one of the fifty-one SOS ODD conversions undertaken by BMMO. In this form the driver had to enter via the saloon and, as per the BMMO norm, sit over the petrol tank. (D. R. Harvey Collection)

Llandudno Royal Blue

CC 6121

Llandudno Royal Blue had six SOS ODDs which were rebuilt from SOS S types. The first two were actually based on Tilling-Stevens TS3 chassis which had been modified to SOS S types prior to bodying in 1924. They were registered CC 4538–4539. The remaining four ODDs were CC 5077, 6121–6122 and 6424 and were genuine SOS S rebuilds. They were all bodied by United with a B26F layout. There are no known photographs of these six Llandudno Royal Blue ODDs but CC 6121 is shown in its original state when new in 1926. (J. Carroll)

The Second Generation of SOS Buses Sold to Other Operators

SOS M – Madam

The next new BMMO chassis, introduced in 1928, was designed to get more women passengers onto buses. The new model was the SOS M in which the M stood for Madam and was equipped with more comfortable seating in an attempt to make the vehicles more use-friendly for women passengers. This was the first SOS chassis to have a dropped-frame chassis frame in which, in order to attract this potential market, the bus had a lower floor line and more luxurious upholstered seats, resulting in the seating capacity being reduced from thirty-seven to thirty-four. After the first two SOS M buses, which had bodies similar to the previous QL model with straight-sided panels and rocker panels, the rest of the QL buses had deeper, curved lower saloon panels. This gave the SOS M a more modern appearance. Although the body still retained the raised porch entrance, the seven-bay body had radial windows and a slightly raked windscreen, although the internal bulkhead partition was omitted for the first time. Yet again the weight of the new model was increased to 4 tons 14 cwt, although the wheelbase remained at 16 feet 7½ inches and there were variations according to individual company specifications.

There were just two M types produced in 1928, both of which went to Midland Red. The following year Midland Red received another forty-seven, but the bulk of the M type production was sold to other SOS operators, with the Carlyle Road factory supplying some 118 vehicles.

BMMO

973 (HA 4913) (Opposite top)
973 (HA 4913) lies over in Leicester Bus Station in the years just after the war. This SOS M had a thirty-four-seat body built by Ransomes and dated from 1929. These were lower than the previous QL model but were the last type of SOS bus to retain the somewhat old-fashioned porch entrance. For the first time the body specification required that the windows had slightly radial top corners, which modernised the appearance of the 'Madams', as did the slightly raked windscreen. 973 was one of seven M types to be withdrawn in 1949. (D. R. Harvey Collection)

1024 (HA 4937) (Above)

An even longer-lived SOS M was 1024 (HA 4937). This bus is standing in Spiceal Street alongside the boundary wall of St Martin's Parish Church in Birmingham's Bull Ring, which for many years was used as a layover parking spot for bus services from routes using Coventry, Stratford and Warwick Roads. This Ransomes-bodied single-decker is seen on a hot summer's day on 21 August 1949 and is parked opposite the main F. W. Woolworth's in the city, a store which was renowned for its creaky, polished wooden floor. The bus is facing the markets area of Birmingham while behind it is 2537 (GHA 972), a war-time Duple-bodied Daimler CWA6 dating from 1944. Beyond this double-decker is the famous Bull Ring, which would survive in this form until about 1960 when it was first redeveloped. (D. Tee)

Northern General

438 (BR 7027) (Above)

Northern General received forty SOS M types in 1929 and all were bodied by Ransomes with a B34F layout. This was part of an order for 100 Ransomes bodies placed by BMMO, with the remaining sixty-five being bodied by Brush. 438 (BR 7027), standing in the garage yard in Gateshead, entered service in May 1929 and survived until 1947 whereafter it was sold as a caravan. The lower-built SOS Ms were much sleeker-looking than the previous QLs being fitted with slightly raked windscreens. In many ways they were similar to the early Leyland 'Lion' LT1s, although the vintage-style radiator rather spoilt the otherwise more modern appearance. (Courtesy Go Ahead Northern)

454 (BR 7043) (Opposite top)

The Northern General Company registered their buses either in Gateshead with CN registration letters or with County Durham with UP and less commonly from the same source the letters PT. CU, a South Shields mark, was also employed but the Sunderland-allocated BR seems only to have been used between 1926 and 1930. The SOS Ms were the last batch of NGT buses to have been allocated Sunderland registrations at this time. 454 (BR 7043), a Ransomes-bodied bus was rebuilt with the rather unattractive roof-mounted roller blind destination boxes, which in this case appear not to be in use. The lowered bodywork of SOS Ms were rather spoilt by this 1930s addition which seemed to make the juxtaposition of the narrow cab and the wide, low radiator completely out of kilter with the rest of the vehicle. 454 entered service in July 1929 and was sold eighteen years later in July 1947. The body now no longer looks modern as the bus stands awaiting its next duty in about 1946. (W. J. Haynes)

Potteries Motor Traction

159 (VT 2508) (Above)

Potteries Motor Traction's twenty-five SOS Ms all received Brush B34F bodies. Numbered 152–176 with consecutive registrations VT 2501–2525, a line-up of five M types is led by 159 (VT 2508) and next to it 157 (VT 2506). The Brush-bodies were virtually identical to those built on the M model by Ransomes but somehow just looked lower. All of the PMT M types were withdrawn during 1937 and 1938, but 159 did escape the breakers' torch as it was sold to a showman for further use. (R. Marshall Collection)

168 (VT 2517) (Above)
SOS M 168 (VT 2517), stands in St Thomas Place alongside the Marquis of Granby public house in the centre of Penkhull. The bus is facing the St Thomas's Church and its churchyard. Penkhull was developed by Herbert Minton, the famous ceramic tile-manufacturer, as a dormitory suburb of Stoke when the ecclesiastical parish was created out of the parish of Stoke in 1844. 168 was one of a batch of twenty-five Brush-bodied SOS Ms bought in 1929. They were not a long-lived group of buses as they were all withdrawn by 1938, although nine of them were sold for use as showman's vehicles. No such luck befell 168, which was broken up by a Hanley scrap merchant named Lewis. (Commercial Postcard)

Trent Motor Traction
405 (CH 8111) (Opposite top)
Leading a group of three SOS types in July 1930 is 405 (CH 8111). This SOS M was fitted with a Brush B34F body and dated from 1929. Behind it is an unidentifiable SOS Q, distinguishable from the M by being considerably taller, having artillery front wheels and therefore no front-wheel brakes and cycle-style front mudguards. On the extreme right is 410 (CH 8121), which on this obviously hot day, is parked with the centre emergency exit wide open in an attempt to cool down the saloon. They were all parked at the George Garage at Langworth just east of Lincoln on the A158 and are obviously on their way back from Skegness. From here the two leading buses will go their separate ways, with 405 going to Derby and the Q returning to Nottingham. (G. H. F. Atkins, courtesy J. Banks)

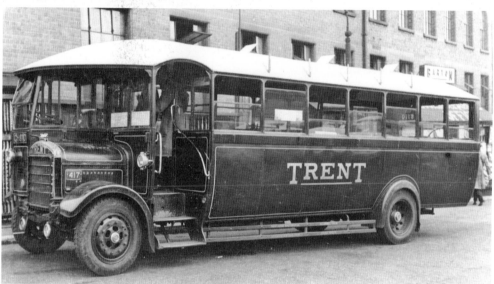

417 (CH 8110) (Above)

There were thirty SOS Ms delivered to Trent Motor Traction in 1929. One of these, 417 (CH 8110), is parked in Huntingdon Street Bus Station in Nottingham just beyond the newspaper stall. All but the last five had Short B34F bodies and like the Midland Red examples were only fitted with destination stencils buried deep against the front bulkhead in the recess of the engine half-cab rather than a front-canopy destination box. The six-bay construction body, (plus the square, rear-most side windows), was a very neat-looking affair with curved steel body panelling, a porch entrance and three fairly manageable steps into the saloon. Still of lightweight construction, these 'Madams' still only weighed about 4.75 tons, which was no mean feat as the bodies were wider, longer and better equipped than previous types of SOS single-deckers. The short length of the engine bay reflects the size of the compact four-cylinder engine. Once again these Ms were not long-lived, mostly being sold off in 1938. (W. J. Haynes)

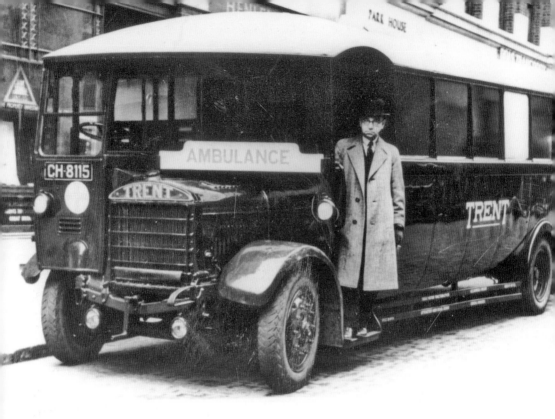

407 (CH 8115) (Above)
Those Trent SOS Ms which survived the withdrawals of 1938 were converted into ambulances in 1939. 407 (CH 8115) was one of the first ten so treated. This conversion was carried out as part of the Emergency Powers Act and the vehicles were placed under the powers of the Regional Transport Commissioner for the North Midlands region. The Chairman of the Commission was Mr J. H. Stirk, who is standing on the step. The conversion involved removing all the seats and building a pair of metal frames on both sides of the gangway. These frames carried two rows of five stretchers as well as two 'walking wounded'. Some of the windows were painted over while in this case the fourth window appears to have just been boarded over. Access to the ambulance was via the central rear emergency exit. It remained as an ambulance until about 1945. (Trent M. T.)

403 (CH 8105) (Opposite top)
This is how many old SOS buses finished up! Trent's former 403 (CH 8105) became a showman's caravan. With smoke coming out of the stove-pipe chimney, many of the windows in the saloon have been panelled over and, providing the bodywork was well maintained and remained watertight, these old buses provided a cosy mobile home for workers working in travelling circuses and fairgrounds. CH 8105 was used as a caravan, judging by the curtains in the three remaining windows. (D. R. Harvey Collection)

Ortona

32 (VE 501) (Above)

The first of the quintet of Ortona SOS Ms, 32 (VE 501) has been parked to show off its lower three-stepped entrance as well as the internal bulkhead arrangement with the flywheel housing just intruding onto the saloon floor line. The radial saloon windows, raked windscreen and curved body panels give the bus a much more sleek appearance. These buses were fast, economical and reliable and were quite the equal of contemporary Leyland 'Tiger TS1 etc. and the recently introduced AEC 'Regal', although their old-style radiators and porch entrances made them look a lot older than they actually were! (East Anglia TM)

72 (VE 502) (Above)

Ortona's last purchase of the SOS marque was five M types, of which the first two were bodied by Brush whereas the last three had Ransomes bodies. They were all delivered between March and May 1929. Like their contemporary Trent equivalents, the five Ortona buses were converted into ambulances at the outbreak of the Second World War. VE 502 was the second of the Brush-bodied pair and after acquisition by Eastern Counties as their SM72 it lasted in service until 1939. It was a strange thing but these 'Madams' looked quite up to date when they were new as in this case, but within five years the buses were somehow transformed into something quite ancient without actually being altered! (D. R. Harvey Collection)

Peterborough Electric

M3 (FL7511) (Opposite top)

The SOS Ms were the swan-song of SOS purchases by Peterborough Electric when twelve Brush-bodied buses entered service between March and May 1929. PET had been first registered on 5 August 1902 to operate tramcars in the City as part of the British Electric Traction Group, but after introducing buses in 1919 the company was taken over by the Tilling Group in May 1928, which meant the end of the association with BMMO chassis. M3 (FL 7511) stands inside the Peterborough garage at the end of the day and gets the time-honoured hose-down before being parked up for the night. (D. R. Harvey Collection)

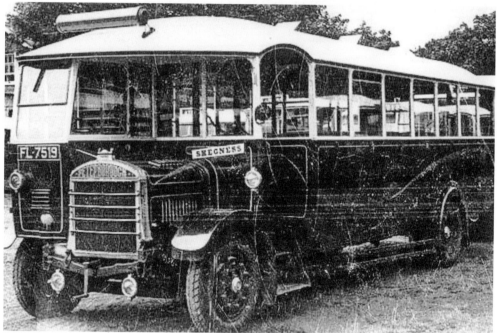

M11 (FL 7519) (Above)

M11 (FL 7519) appears to be parked in Skegness along with other buses and coaches working on excursions to the Lincolnshire seaside resort. It is a measure of the calibre of the SOS M type that the Peterborough Electric Company was prepared to use these buses on extended journeys such as this 'seaside special'. In 1939 this bus, as part of the surviving last seven, was converted into a wartime ambulance and was sold via Bird's dealership, Stratford, to a showman. (D. R. Harvey Collection)

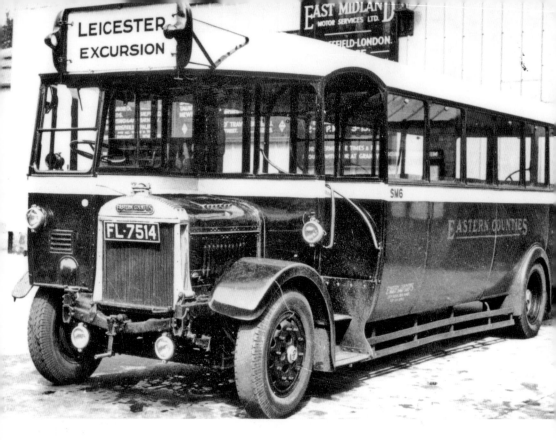

M6 (FL 7514) (Above)

The rebuilding and simplification of the radiator by the Eastern Counties engineers certainly improved the appearance of the former Peterborough Electric SOS M types. By now ECOC's M6 (FL 7514) was fitted with a huge Bible board destination indicator, whose design was at odds with the new radiator. The bus was eventually withdrawn in 1939 and converted into a wartime emergency ambulance. The bus is standing in Peterborough Bus Station and just visible is the Early English tower of the Cathedral, dating from 1340. It became the Cathedral of the new Diocese of Peterborough in 1541 and it is now known as the Cathedral Church of St Peter, St Paul and St Andrew. (D. R. Harvey Collection)

Llandudno Royal Blue

CC 8562 (Opposite top)

Leaving Conway with the impressive medieval castle behind in 1933 is CC8562. This was one of Llandudno Blue's six SOS Ms of 1929. The bus is crossing Thomas Telford's 1826 suspension bridge spanning the River Conway. Telford matched the bridge's supporting towers with the castle's turrets. Construction of Conway Castle began in 1283. The castle was an important part of King Edward I's plan of surrounding Wales in 'an iron ring of castles' to subdue the rebellious population. The bus, by now numbered 534 in the Crosville fleet, is on its way to Llandudno Junction and Llandudno but first has to inch its way through the narrow Gothic portals of the bridge. (D. R. Harvey Collection)

CC 8566 (Above)

One of Llandudno Royal Blue's six SOS Ms waits at the Ransomes factory in Ipswich prior to delivery. Looking very smart in its lined-out blue-and-white livery, the bus weighed exactly 4.5 tons when new. CC 8566 was the 1000th SOS chassis to be constructed since production began in 1923. These six vehicles were the last buses bought by Llandudno Royal Blue, although six ODDs and two QLCs were to follow before the influence of the Crosville ownership – which had purchased the North Wales operator on 18 February 1931 – brought an end to the purchase of SOS chassis in 1930. (B. W. Ware Collection)

SOS RR (Rolls-Royce)

The unsuccessful long-distance SOS XL coaches of 1929 went through a metamorphosis during the following year when the second-hand Carlyle or Brush-built bodies were fitted to a new chassis. The RR type was fitted with the recently introduced RR2LB 6.373 litre six-cylinder petrol engine within the still standard SOS wheelbase of 16 feet 7.5 inches. This new combination was classified RR (Rolls-Royce), and needed the larger, more powerful engine as the all-up unladen weight of the bus was 5 tons 12 cwt. These more powerful coaches were the first SOS vehicles to receive a new design of radiator which was much modern than previous BMMO designs. The remnants of the Tilling-Stevens style of radiator was finally abandoned with a much deeper radiator to match raised bonnet line. The header tank retained the cast name of the operator, though the concave shape of its bottom rather spoilt the design, which was to be retained until deliveries made in 1935. Although none of them were built new for other operators, all fifty of these thirty-seat dual-purpose coaches were sent on loan to Potteries Motor Traction between 1940 and 1945 and only two ever re-entered service, albeit briefly, with Midland Red, the other forty-eight being broken up by PMT.

BMMO
1187 (HA 4958) (Below)
A little like the hammer that has had two heads and three handles but is still the same hammer, the SOS RRs were re-chassied SOS XLs, built and then scrapped in 1929 and then fitted with the year-old coach bodies. The 'new' coaches were fitted with bodies built by either Brush or Ransomes. In this case HA 4958 had a Brush-built body and entered service in this form in 1930. The newly re-styled radiator was a definite improvement from the previous SOS models, while the body styling was reminiscent of Brush bodies built on contemporary Leyland 'Tiger' chassis. HA 4958 is parked behind Digbeth garage in about 1931 when virtually new. (J. Cull)

Potteries Motor Traction

225 (VT 4525) (Top)

Built in 1929, this coach was one of the unsuccessful XL vehicles and had originally been Midland Red's 1083 (HA 4990). This coach was one of a pair, 224–225, which were sent on loan to PMT in 1929. Returned to Carlyle Road and fitted with the new six-cylinder petrol engine, the coach was reclassified as an SOS RR and was re-registered VT 4525, with the fleet number 225 in the PMT fleet. It is in Stoke when first converted into the RR type and is carrying the PET belted garter logo, which was usually found only on coaches. The Brush body was fitted with the curved window on the corner of the bulkhead above the engine bay, which was a briefly popular stylistic feature. (J. Cooke Collection)

224 (VT 4524) (Above)

The prolific inter-war photographer John Cull took this photograph of PMT 224 (VT 4524) in about 1934. The coach is parked in Mill Lane, Digbeth next to the Midland Red garage. The coach had originally been registered HA 4989 but was on loan to PMT when all the SOS XLs were recalled and re-chassied as the RR type. The deep coach-type seating in this Brush C30F-bodied vehicle can be seen just above the saloon waist-rail. The tradition of supplying chassis with the minimum space for the driver and the maximum space for the passengers is well shown in this offside view of 224 (VT 4524). To assist this, the petrol tank was placed in the usual SOS position beneath the seat in the driver's cab. In this condition the coaches lasted until 1936, when they were rebodied by Burlingham and lasted until 1947. (J. Cull)

SOS SRR (Short [bodied] Rolls-Royce)

The successor to the RR was the SRR, which was mechanically the same as the previous model and had a similar-looking body, albeit lower, constructed by Short Brothers again with a C30F layout. Only two were built for Midland Red while the remaining ten were bought by Northern General.

BMMO
1243 (HA 6174) (Below)
There were just two SOS SRR coaches operated by Midland Red. The first of these consecutively numbered coaches was HA 6174 and they had Short Brothers bodies. The bodies had deep roofs and, uniquely for Midland Red's pre-war single-deckers, actually had a roller blind destination box incorporated into the front dome. Midland Red's perversity had the destination display of 'SHREWSBURY' masked by a wooden headboard which displays 'SHREWSBURY VIA RUGBY, COVENTRY AND BIRMINGHAM'. The coach has the red livery with maroon bands and roof and is waiting in Pool Meadow Bus Station in Coventry in August 1939, having already travelled the 36 miles from Northampton on this long X96 stage carriage service. Both Midland Red SRRs were on loan to Potteries from 1940 until 1944 but it is doubtful if either operated again on their return to the parent company. (R. T. Coxon)

Northern General
480 (CN 4247) (Opposite top)
The ten SOS SRR coaches for Northern General were numbered 472–481. They entered service during July and August 1930 and were fitted with Short Brothers C30F bodies. These bodies were a good deal sleeker in appearance to the previous RR model with deeper panelling and, for the first time in the Northern General SOS fleet, a single-line destination box. These ten coaches were bought for the Newcastle-on-Tyne to Liverpool service with intermediate stops as shown on the cantrail slip board. It must have been an interesting journey in 1930. Seven of the coaches were rebuilt in 1936 when they were

reseated to C31F. All of the coaches remained in service until July 1940, whereupon they were impressed by the War Department. (Courtesy of Go Ahead Northern)

481 CN 4248 (Above)
Northern General's ten SOS SRRs, numbered 472–481, were the first SOS-built vehicles to be fitted with roller-blind destination indicators. The ten Short Brothers-bodied thirty-seater coaches were in July and August 1930 specifically for the Newcastle-on-Tyne to Liverpool service which had been introduced two years earlier. The original bodywork was beginning to look a little antiquated by the mid-1930s and so seven of them, including 481 (CN 4248), were rebuilt during 1936 in order to modernise their appearance. This entailed lowering the side panels, adding streamlined wings, modifying the livery with some Art Deco-styling lines and upgrading the seating both in terms of luxuriousness and capacity, which went up to C31F. 481 is working on the regular service to Blackpool via Barnard Castle and Lancaster sometime after it was rebuilt. Rebuilt or not, all ten were requisitioned by the Ministry of War Transport in July 1940. After war service, 481 was briefly sent to BMMO as their 2528 in January 1943, before being returned immediately to NGT with a new fleet number of 1048, although it only lasted until the end of 1945. (C. W. Routh)

SOS COD

This was based on the dual-purpose XL chassis but fitted with a bus body. The body of the bus was a further development of the standard Midland Red style. For the first time the body only had five bays and the porch entrance, which had previously been standard, disappeared with the COD model. The nominal designer of the bus was Mr P. G. Stone-Clarke, who was chief engineer of Trent Motor Traction. There were sixty-one SOS CODs built, of which sixty were the four-cylinder petrol-engined model. BMMO received twenty-two CODs in 1930 but like the XL model before it the Midland Red examples were rebuilt as the new IM4 type and were given new bodies built by Short Brothers. This eliminated the COD type within just over a year as a type operated by Midland Red. The single missing chassis was the COD six-cylinder vehicle registered HA 5007, which entered service in 1930 and was quickly rebuilt into an SOS MM type by the end of that year. The remaining thirty-eight vehicles were bodied by Brush with B34F units, with Potteries Motor Traction receiving twenty-one and Trent Motor Traction having seventeen, all being fitted with the new flat-topped radiator.

BMMO

1088 (HA 5007)
The prototype SOS COD was built in 1930 and was fitted by Carlyle with their own B34F body, distinguishable by the D-shaped rear side windows. The bus was fitted with the six-cylinder 6.373 litre engine, but unlike the examples sold to Potteries and Trent, this bus was converted to MM specification and served as the prototype for Midland Red's ten Ransomes-bodied buses which would, after 1944, be numbered 1136–1145. HA 5007, despite its unhappy beginnings, in its new guise, remained in service until 1949. (Midland Red)

1153 (HA 6158)

Seen on 8 October 1949 just a few weeks before its withdrawal, HA 6158, by now numbered 1153, was one of the twenty-two production SOS CODs built in 1930 which were rebodied within a year of entry into service by Short Brothers. The bus was reclassified as an IM4 and had a B34F layout. The bus is standing in Market Street, Ashby-de-la-Zouch and is going on the 5-mile-long 699 route to Overseal, which is the southernmost settlement in Derbyshire, on the border with Leicestershire. (D. Tee)

Potteries Motor Traction

204 (VT 4504)

Posed at Carlyle Road Works, Edgbaston, Birmingham when new in 1930 is SOS COD 204 (VT 4504). The design of the Brush body had again developed, as it eliminated for the first time the raised Gothic porch and it reduced the numbers down to six from seven bays. When new the buses had side slip boards as well as a destination board across the front bulkhead. The only jarring design feature was ironically the very feature which in 1930 was considered modern, namely the half-covered rear-wheel arch. This bus was requisitioned for use as an ambulance between 1940 and 1945 but was not deemed economically viable to re-enter PSV service and was broken up by the company. (J. Cooke Collection)

216 (VT 4516)

Photographs of a driver squeezing himself into the cramped cab of an SOS vehicle are extremely rare. The door was hinged at the front corner of the cab, which meant the driver climbed into the cab and then sat down behind the door and of course on top of the petrol tank. Potteries Motor Traction's 216 (VT 4516), one of that company's twenty-one Brush-bodied SOS CODs, stands in Newcastle-under-Lyme's Iron Market. Towering above it is the Municipal Hall, built between 1888 and 1890 to commemorate the Golden Jubilee of Queen Victoria. Alas, this piece of wonderful Victorian architectural rhubarb was demolished in 1967. (J. Cooke Collection)

Trent Motor Traction

458 (CH 8908) (Above)
The SOS COD was a variation of the SOS M, whose lower-slung Brush-built body was also enhanced by reducing the number of bays from seven to six. The appearance of the thirty-four-seat body was also improved by having the rear bay subtly curved at the bottom. The CODs were the first SOS vehicles to have the new-styled flat-topped radiator. Although a great improvement on the previous type, the new style with the larger header tank embossed with the fleet name 'TRENT' looked slightly dated even when first introduced, but continued as the SOS standard until 1938. When new in May 1930, SOS COD 458 (CH 8908) was painted in the usual red livery but with the waist-rail picked out in a deeper shade of the same colour. Two years later the bus was renumbered 208. (Potteries Motor Traction)

465 (CH 8915) (Opposite top)
When new, the Trent SOS COD buses were used when required on excursion and limited-stop work. At the time, the company hardly had anything else to use on such rotas and so the comfortable seating on the new buses would have been most welcome for the passengers. 465 (CH 8915), by this time just fifteen months old, seems to be doing good business as it waits in a damp-looking Nottingham bus station in August 1931 prior to leaving on a limited-stop service to Skegness. The conductor, standing next to the woman standing with her back towards the photographer, is looking at the passenger list before allocating the spares in the vehicle. The bus is still not equipped with roof destination slip boards as the metal supports are exposed. This bus was renumbered during the following year as 215 and survived with Trent until 1940, whereupon it was impressed by the War Department and was subsequently written off by them. (G. H. F. Atkins, courtesy J. Banks)

452 (CH 8902) (Above)
The conductor of Trent SOS COD 452 (CH 8902), delivered in June 1930, stands alongside his Brush-bodied charge with the signal box near the former Chellaston and Swarkestone railway station in the background. Swarkestone stands on the River Trent and it was here that during the Jacobite Rebellion in 1745 the advance party of Bonnie Prince Charlie's army reached the most southerly point of their advance on London before retreating back to Derby and returning back to Scotland before their final disastrous defeat at the Battle of Culloden. (D. R. Harvey Collection)

SOS IM4 (Improved Madam Four-Cylinder)

The two Improved Madam prototypes entered service in 1929 and were allocated to Midland Red and Northern General respectively, while one of the thirty-nine MMs converted to IM4 specification in 1930 was sold to Potteries Motor Traction. The IM4 model was the last of the SOS chassis to be built with the original 4.344 litre SOS petrol engine and was a development of the SOS MM and the COD type. The body had deep, curved side-panels and a straight nearside roof-line which eliminated any semblance of a porch roof over the three-step entrance. The earliest of the buses had the large header tank atop the radiator and were the last SOS buses to have the four decorative horizontal bars on the radiator, which seemed to be a last hurrah to the old Tilling-Stevens buses. The buses were 26 feet 2 inches long and 7 feet 4½ inches wide, but were higher at 9 feet 6 inches and weighed about 4 tons 12 cwt. The 1933 deliveries had a more modern appearance, being of five-bay construction rather than the previous six, with radial saloon windows with half-drop opening windows and no roof overhang above the windscreen. These later buses were weighted about two hundredweight more and were classified as IM4Ds. The SOS IM4 was in production between 1931 and 1933 and represented a real advance on previous models. The two prototypes had Carlyle B34F bodies while the 1931 and 1933 IM4s, which numbered 138 buses, had Short B34F bodies. The eighty-one vehicles built in 1932 had Brush bodies. A total of eighty-nine IM4s were sold to other BET operators.

BMMO

1279 (HA 6201) (Opposite above)
Standing in Smallbrook Street in central Birmingham in about 1935 is HA 6201. This Short-bodied SOS IM4 single-decker entered service four years earlier and is working on the 16-mile-long 147 route to Redditch via Alvechurch. The bodywork on the IM4s had single-piece, slightly curved side body panels, all of which were of the same length and lower than on previous bodies. These Short Brothers-bodied IM4s had deep-domed roofs which made them easily distinguishable from the contemporary Brush-bodied examples. The bus has two large sidelights while the headlights are below the radiator in the position usually used for spotlights. This petrol-engined bus had a long career, not being withdrawn until 1950. (Warwickshire Local Studies Collection)

1330 (HA 8257) (Opposite below)
Parked in Coalville on Saturday 8 October 1949 is 1330 (HA 8257). This SOS IM4 had a Brush B34F body and entered service in 1931. Both the Brush- and the Short-bodied IM4s had three roof ventilators which are open on this bus. The composite constructions of the Brush bodies were fractionally lower than the metal-framed Short Brothers examples, but had deeper saloon windows with very square rear dome side windows. Clearly visible is the strangely located cab door, which was hung onto the offside corner of the cab. (D. Tee)

1461 (HA 8356) (Above)
A final batch of thirty SOS IM4s was received by Midland Red in late 1933 and early
1934. All were bodied by Short Brothers in a more modern style that was distinctly more
rounded and lacked the overhanging front dome, so that it was flush to the top of the
windscreen. This body design rather looked forward to those fitted to the 1934 SOS
ONs. With its back wheel chocked with a brick, 1461 (HA 8356) is parked in between
duties on the 704 service from Burton to Ashby on 8 October 1949. (D. Tee)

Northern

542 (CN 4742) (Opposite top)
542 (CN 4742) was one of the ten SOS IM4s delivered to Northern General in March
1931. NGT had received one IM4 in the previous year and all of them had received Short
B34F bodywork. When new these were the first Northern buses to be fitted with route
number indicators, which were mounted on the front bulkhead underneath the canopy.
This proved to be a fairly unsatisfactory arrangement. The response was to replace these
with a small roller blind destination blind set in the canopy. For the intending passenger,
the single-line destination was about as distinguishable as the half-hidden route number,
hidden away in the gloom of the half-cab! 542 remained largely unaltered after this,
except for being fitted with sliding saloon ventilation windows, and was withdrawn in
1950 as one of the last four IM4s in service. Sister vehicle 540, a bus which was operated
by Bensham garage in Gateshead, had been withdrawn in 1950 and converted into a
caravan and parked at a site at Ellington, Northumberland. It was moved to the North of
England Open Air Museum at Beamish in May 1972 and stored under a tarpaulin until
work began on restoring it in November 2009. (R. Marshall)

HA 8253 (Above)

Making an interesting comparison to Northern's 542, 1041 (HA 8253) was one of two former Midland Red SOS IM4s that finished their careers with the Tyneside operator. This Brush-bodied example entered service in March 1932 and was impressed by the War Department in 1940. It was returned to Northern General in 1942 where it was operated for another eight years. Obviously lacking a front destination box, the subtle changes in the interpretation of the body specification, such as the curved top to the porch and canopy and the slightly radial saloon windows, gave a slightly less austere look to these former Midland Red buses. (D. R. Harvey Collection)

Potteries Motor Traction

179 (VT 7905) (Above)

Loading up with passengers in Colwyn Bay are a pair of SOS IM4s, both operated by the Potteries Motor Traction group, but both are quite different vehicles. The leading bus is PMT's 179 (VT 7905), which was bodied by Brush in May 1932 as one the six which entered the main fleet. The vehicle behind is VT 6155, one of the IM4s operated by four of the associated operators which were acquired in 1928 by PET and absorbed into the parent PMT fleet in 1932. All of these twelve IM4s were bodied by Short Brothers. VT 6155 was originally owned by W & F Rogerson of Burslem and these Short-bodied buses could be distinguished from the Brush-bodied vehicles by a different offside cab window layout. (D. R. Harvey Collection)

Trent Motor Traction

227 (CH 9923) (Opposite above)

Standing in Huntingdon Street Bus Station in Nottingham when about three years old, this Short-bodied SOS IM4 of 1931 was one of twelve of the type delivered that year. 227 (CH 9923), originally numbered 477, had bodywork which was very similar to the earlier SOS CODs and MMs. The brackets on the roof cantrail were intended to carry advertising boards but frequently they were not used and eventually fell out of use. The bus still has its rear mudguard covers and is still in the original red livery with a darker waist-rail band. (W. J. Haynes)

253 (RC 538) (Opposite below)

Standing in Huntingdon Street in Nottingham is a brand-new Brush-bodied SOS IM4. The Brush bodies differed from the Short-bodied equivalents with the rear side window at the back of the saloon being slightly sloped and therefore a little shapelier. As if to emphasise their credentials as 'Improved Madams', the interior was given a more colourful and cheerful appearance, with the previous drab brown seating giving way to plum leather upholstery. Interestingly, the intermediate model between the M 'Madam' and the 'Improved Madams' (IM4s), which was the MM, (Modified Madam), was not supplied by BMMO to any of its outside operators. (W. J. Haynes)

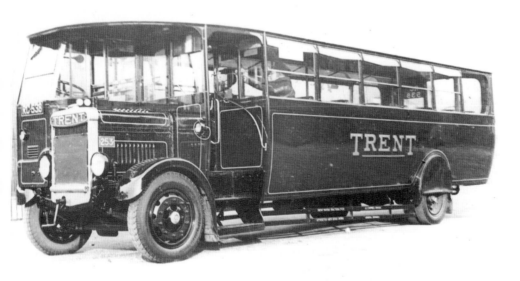

235 (RC 410) (Above)
This was one of the twenty-five Brush-bodied SOS IM4s delivered to Trent in June 1932, but 235 (RC 410) was one of a quartet of Trent SOS IM4s to have a surprisingly interesting 'afterlife'. In 1947 Mountain Transport Services of Chelsea purchased RC 408–410 and RC 426. Between October 1947 and August 1949 London Transport hired a large quantity of buses and coaches from independent operators to supplement their bus fleet as there was a chronic shortage of new buses. They were allocated to Hammersmith, Mortlake and Putney Bridge garages from April 1948 until April 1949. Former 235 (RC 410) was allocated to the latter garage, where it was often found working on the 74 route from Baker Street to Putney via Marble Arch, South Kensington and Earl's Court. (A. P. Newland)

276 (RC 1295) (Opposite above)
The final four-cylinder SOS type buses to be delivered to Trent were twenty-five IM4s delivered in 1933. 276 (RC 1295), painted in the usual smart red livery but with a dark-red waistband, stands in Huntingdon Street Bus Station in Nottingham awaiting its next turn of duty. This vehicle had a Short Brothers B34F body which benefited from having window pans with corners which were very slightly radial, although as to whether the rear wheel spats actually improved the appearance of these buses is debatable. As they slowed down tyre replacement and routine maintenance on the back axle and brakes, the spats were taken off these buses, which also improved the air flow over the brake pads. (D. R. Harvey Collection)

256 (RC 541) (Opposite below)
Some SOS buses ended their days as static caravans and a few of the marque owe their preservation to their survival as these humble holiday homes. Former Trent 256 (RC 541), a Brush-bodied SOS IM4 delivered in July 1932, stands on the side of the open moorland near to the village of Saddleworth in the Lancashire Pennines in June 1954, but alas failed to last long enough to be worthy of saving. The obligatory coal-fired stove coupled to

the tall chimney provided both heat and cooking facilities, while toilet facilities were in the shed to the left. Providing the static caravan was well maintained and painted, the wooden bodies could last for several decades and provided their owners with a 'home from home' in the countryside. (N. R. Knight)

Tynemouth & District (*No photograph*)

There were only two SOS IM4s delivered to the Tynemouth & District Company. They were numbered T61 and T62 with registrations FT 2848 and 2849. They had Short B34F bodies and entered service in 1933 but only lasted a year with the company before passing to the General County Omnibus Company of Chester-le-Street as their 49 and 50.

SOS IM6 (Improved Madam Six-Cylinder)

This was the first large-scale production SOS model to have the six-cylinder 5.986 litre SOS RR2SB engine and the SOS IM6 single-decker was produced concurrently with the IM4 chassis. These buses were fitted with a new crash gearbox which had a 'silent third' gear. The new flat-topped radiator introduced on the IM4s were used but were longer in order to cool the larger engine. Although the first of the BMMO IM6s were fitted with Brush bodies taken from the SOS COD types, those supplied to operators elsewhere were constructed by Short Brothers with a B34F layout, a deep-roofed six-bay body and weighed about 4 tons 17 cwt with a height of 9 feet 3 inches.

BMMO

1315 (HA 6245) (Opposite above)
One of the first batch of SOS IM6s, 1315 (HA 6245) was one of twenty-two of these Brush-bodied six-cylinder petrol-engined buses which entered service in 1931. The taller bonnet line of the IM6 is clearly visible, though the ventilation slats on the bonnet side have been replaced by a long cowling which was usually associated with much later SON types. Lying over in Frome in about 1948, the bodywork has been rebuilt with a continuous metal rain strip above the saloon windows, giving the body an almost utility appearance. Behind the bus is a public house which is tied to Stroud Ales. 1315 had an eventful life as it was impressed by the War Department in 1940 and after its return in 1942 was converted during the following year to run on producer gas from Evesham garage. In order to comply with the MoWT edict that up to 10 per cent of a large petrol-engined bus fleet would have to be converted to run on producer gas, Midland Red simply converted the Evesham garage bus fleet to this fuel substitute, leaving the rest of the operating area to operate normally. A cunning and successful plan! (R. K. Blencowe)

1317 (HA 7327) (Opposite below)
1317 (HA 7327) is operating much nearer its home! The bus is pulling away from the war-time bus shelters opposite Lightwoods Park, Bearwood and is about to begin the climb up to the Warley Cinema where it will turn onto Wolverhampton Road, where it could make up time on the 125 service to Dudley. These SOS IM6s, with their six-cylinder petrol engines, would have been quite useful on the hilly roads around the Black Country. The bus is seen in about 1948, but unlike 1315, it appears to have retained its glass saloon rain shields. (A. N. Porter)

1426 (HA 8301) (Above)

Parked in Evesham High Street's bus station in front of the Old Swan Inn is SOS IM6 1426 (HA 8301). This vehicle had a Short B34F body and belonged to the last group of twenty-eight of the type that were built in 1933. It still carries the vestiges of the central vertical chrome strip on the radiator, which originally would have carried the letters SOS below the radiator header tank. Without any destination gear it is difficult to believe that this bus was effectively one of the same batch as the Northern General vehicles which immediately followed on from these Midland Red IM6s. 1426 was also converted to run on producer gas in 1943 and 1944 and was one of seventeen of this class to operate from Evesham garage to be so converted. (S. N. J. White)

Northern General

578 (CN 5473) (Opposite top)

Northern General received two batches of ten IM6s in 1931 and 1933, both of which were bodied by Short Brothers. The 1931 batch was numbered 546–555 (CN 4746–4755) while the second ten were numbered 576–585 (CN 5471–5480). 578 (CN 5473), from the second group of 1933, was chosen by Short for their official photographic archive and was posed alongside the outer stone wall of Rochester Castle on the Esplanade above the River Medway in 1933. The most noticeable difference between the IM4s and the IM6s was the slightly longer bonnet to accommodate the six-cylinder 5.986 litre SOS RR2SB engine and deeper radiator. The only jarring note of the design was the disproportionately large destination box, which although much better than the old slip board arrangement on previous SOS models operated by Northern, was a perhaps a little too much! (Short Brothers)

550 (CN 4750) (Above)

The Wishaw-based railway wagon body-builder returned to bus body-building in 1946, basically for two operating groups. The Red and White built over fifty rather austere single-deck bodies on Albion 'Valkyrie' CX13 chassis, while for the Northern General group they rebodied over seventy pre-war AEC 'Regal' o662s and SOS IM6s. 550 (CN 4750) stands alongside a post-war Guy 'Arab' III with a Brush B38F body in Newcastle which was specially designed to replicate the concept of maximising body space and having the shortest possible engine bay. The SOS IM6 exhibits this feature and also shows off its very austere Pickering B34F body. By now renumbered 998, the rebodying of this IM6 took place in 1949 and extended the life of this bus until 1955. (D. R. Harvey Collection)

580 (CN 5475)

580 (CN 5475), dating from May 1933, belonged to the second batch of Northern General's SOS IM6s. Nearly all of Northern's BMMO built buses were impressed by the Ministry of Transport for the War Department in July 1940 but all but a few were returned to NGT in the spring and summer of 1942. 580 received a new, very utilitarian body built by Pickering with B34F body in 1947 and was renumbered 1025 and would survive until 1955. Pickering were based in Wishaw in Lanarkshire and were basically railway wagon- and carriage-builders who, like many similar companies, such as Charles Roberts, Cravens, Birmingham RCW and Gloucester RCW, when they were short of work, filled up their order book by constructing bus bodies. Pickering were at their most active in the bus body-building trade from 1938 until 1950. (D. R. Harvey Collection)

Trent

120 (CH 9900)

The sixteen SOS IM6s of 1931 were numbered 120–135 (CH 9900–9915), and were among the last Trent vehicles to be registered by Derby County Council. The SOS IM6s had deeper radiators than the earlier IM4 model and the radiator projected slightly beyond the cab apron. Former Trent 130 (CH 9910) was impressed by the War Department in 1940 and was numbered M1261760 before being sold to Midland Red via the WD's store at Ashchurch in 1942. It was then numbered 2473 in the Midland Red fleet and is seen parked at an unknown location with numerous patched-up body panels and a sagging waist-rail in about 1948. (D. R. Harvey Collection)

138 (RC 903)

The lady with a stylish summer hat strides purposefully behind 138 (RC 903) as it stands in the newly constructed Derby Bus Station. In 1933 a final ten IM6s were purchased from BMMO. These buses had Short B34F bodies and were built for use on the company's longer stage carriage services. The IM6 chassis could be distinguished from the four-cylinder IM4s by having longer radiators to match the deeper bonnets required by the larger engine. The bodywork followed the usual Short Brothers design and, being metal-framed, was remarkably long-lived. (C. W. Routh)

141 (RC 906)

A virtually new 141 (RC 906) is parked in Huntingdon Street Bus Station in Nottingham. Coming in from the north-west of Nottingham from Gedling, the Short-bodied SOS IM6 still has its rear-wheel mudguard spats. It is obviously a hot summer's day as all the windows are pulled right down. The IM6 also displays the much more shallow steps in the porch entrance, revealing just how the SOS chassis development had, over the years, reduced the chassis and floor height of these Birmingham-built buses. These buses were purchased by Trent because their larger, smooth-running 5.986 litre petrol engines, coupled to a still fairly lightweight body construction, were well suited to the longer services operated in the Trent Valley by the company.
(D. R. Harvey Collection)

Sunderland District *(No photograph)*

There were only four SOS IM6s delivered to the Sunderland District Company. They were numbered 100–103 with registrations UP 5501–5504. They entered service in 1931 and were fitted with Short B32F bodies and although painted in the Sunderland District blue-and-off-white livery, they looked very similar to the IM6s of Northern General. The four buses were withdrawn over a nine-year period, with 100 being impressed by the Ministry of Supply while the last pair, 103 and 101, were withdrawn in 1948 and 1949 respectively.

Later SOS Types and the Gradual Decline in Popularity

Year	BMMO Chassis Type	BMMO	Northern	Tyne mouth	PMT	Trent	Llandudno Blue	Ortona	Peterb.	Wakefields	Sund land
	ON	33	12			10				2	12
	DON	3									
	FEDD	50									
	REDD				15						
	LRR	5			1						
	REC	1									
	ON	50				6					
	LRR	25									
	OLR	25									
	DON	49				30					
	SON	1									
	FEDD	85				15					
	DON					40					
	ON					6					
	SON	65									
	FEDD	50									
	REC	3									
	SLR	50									
	SON	100									
	FEDD	50									
	SON	50									
	FEDD	50									
	ONC	24				6					
	LON	1									
	SON	38				12					
	FEDD	50									
	SON	50				14					

The reason why, after 1934, BMMO cut back so severely on manufacturing chassis for other BET companies is rather open to conjecture. Almost certainly the main factor was the lack of capacity to supply large numbers of chassis at Carlyle Road Works. Between 1923 and 1933 the total production figures of SOS chassis numbered 1,865, of which 787 chassis were sold to seven BET operators. However, looking at the production figures it is clear that sales to other operators began to decline rapidly after 1929 as only 200 chassis were sold between 1929 and 1933. After 1929 no chassis were sold to either Ortona or Peterborough Electric while in 1930 the last two chassis, a pair of QLCs, were delivered to Llandudno Blue, although the reason for this was the takeover of the two East Anglian companies by Eastern Counties and Llandudno Blue's acquisition by Crosville MS. From 1934 until 1940 BMMO manufactured some 1,080 chassis, of which 808 were for their own use. Once the 1934 orders to the Northern General Group for twenty-six chassis, to Potteries for sixteen chassis (including fifteen REDD double-deckers) and to Trent Motor Traction for ten single-deckers was completed, the only chassis supplied to another operator were those for Trent, who purchased 133 chassis. These Trent vehicles however had bodies supplied to the specification of the operator, rather than previously when complete buses were supplied by BMMO with Midland Red-specification bodies.

The large production of buses for 'home' consumption by Midland Red was due to the sheer number of services being introduced, the replacement of vehicles belonging to the large number of small operators being taken over in the mid- and late 1930s, plus the acquisition of several large operations. For example the Leicester & District Company was taken over on 1 November 1936, which was the culmination of a huge increase in the number of bus services in the Leicester area taken over from other operators.

Thus Carlyle Road Works was not only having to supply the need for large numbers of new buses for its own operating company, but was having to set up and maintain a large overhaul programme, further restricting their capacity to take on further orders for new vehicles from external bus companies.

The other mitigating factor was that the lack of orthodoxy in the design of SOS chassis and the cost of small-scale production of these vehicles inevitably began to price out the company's products, especially compared to the prices of chassis being offered by specialist bus chassis constructors. The increasing popularity of the AEC 'Regal', Bristol's JO range, the Daimler COG5 and the Leyland 'Tiger' TS range was quickly taken up by most of the bus operators to whom BMMO had previously supplied chassis. These manufacturers also began to offer either their own oil engines or, as in the case of Bristol and Daimler, to supply chassis with the Gardner LW type of oil engine at least two years before the BMMO oil engine appeared as a production unit. So by about 1933, BMMO management were taking the radical step to basically close down the manufacturing of bus chassis for other companies, although the Trent Company was kept 'within the fold' to some extent because they had close operational and personnel links with Midland Red.

By 1934, a new, second generation of half-cab single-decker buses was introduced. With their six-cylinder compact, short-length petrol engines, silent third gearbox, longer wheelbase and the body-length increased to 27 feet 6 inches, they had a seating capacity of thirty-eight and were the forerunner of some 583 buses based on the new chassis. A whole new family was developed quickly, introducing a new range of buses fitted with Diesel oil engines. In 1934 the DON-type was introduced using the AEC 7.58 litre oil engine while from 1935 onwards, Midland Red developed its own oil engine. Known as the 'K' type, it was an 8.028 litre engine and was noted for its smooth-running performance. Single-deck buses fitted with this BMMO engine were classified as the SON type while ON types were converted in about 1936 and were classified CONs, for Converted ON type. The last half-cab single-deckers built for BMMO were delivered with GHA registrations in 1939 and were bodied, just like some of the early 'S' types, by Brush of Loughborough who remained a regular body-builder for Midland Red until they ceased production in 1952. The very last SOS SONs, however, were fourteen chassis supplied to Trent Motor Traction which were bodied by Willowbrook and supplied in early 1940.

Similarly, in 1932 a new rear-entrance double-decker bus was introduced. Four of the fifty-four SOS REDDs built during that year were sold to Potteries Motor Traction. Although only seventy REDDs were built in 1934, another fifteen were built. These were the final ones to be constructed and were sold to Potteries. All of the Potteries double-deckers were built with lowbridge bodies. The REDD model was superseded after the construction of a prototype in 1933 by the SOS FEDD. This front-entrance double-decker went into production in 1934 and by the autumn of 1939 some 350 of these impressive buses were built, of which Trent Motor Traction received fifteen buses originally intended for Midland Red.

SOS REDD (Rear Entrance Double-Decker)

The prototype double-decker represented the end product of about eight years of the genesis of the SOS. marque. In 1931, a modified version of the IM6 single-decker chassis was constructed, but with a much shorter 15-foot 7-inch-long wheelbase to suit a double-deck body. The bus was built upon SOS chassis 1541. It was registered HA 7329 and given the BMMO 'A' fleet number 1319. It had cost £1,770 to build, which was about double the corresponding IM4 or IM6 single-decker cost. HA 7329 had a drop-frame rear extension for a rear platform and when fitted with a body, it was 25 feet 3 inches long. It was fitted with the RR 2 LB (long bore), 6.373 litre six-cylinder, side-valve petrol engine and one of the newly introduced 'silent third' gearboxes, designed especially to take the extra torque of the larger engines. The 'silent' third gear was developed to take the drive through helical gears so that the end result was a more melodious than gears which became worn and raspy. The complete bus with an H24/24R layout was bodied by Short Brothers of Rochester in Kent.

The fifty production buses built for Midland Red were built to an overall length of 25 feet 11 inches; as a result the wheelbase length was increased to 16 feet 1½ inches. The production REDDs had the same RR2 LB, 6.373 litre engine as the prototype and retained the 'silent third' helical spur crash gearbox. The Midland Red REDDs were all highbridge buses, and were built to an H26/26R format, which was four more than that on the prototype. The body contract for this first and only production batch of REDDs for Midland Red was awarded to four different body builders. These were Brush, Eastern Counties, Short Brothers and Metro-Cammell.

It is perhaps rather forgotten that Potteries Motor Traction was the only other operator to order the REDD chassis. Their order in 1932 was for four Brush L26/26R-bodied

REDDs, numbered 27–30, (VT 8601–8604), whose chassis numbers, 1644/1647/1653 and 1661 were interspersed with the fifty double-deckers for Midland Red. They were the first new top-covered double-deckers operated by the PMT company and were allocated to operate on the Burslem to Tunstall and Longton to Hanley services.

The 1934 PMT order for REDDs had the succeeding chassis numbers to the first FEDDs, in the 1926–1940 series. Of these fifteen, the twelve numbered 232–243 (AVT 552–563), received Short Brothers bodies, though in this case had an L30/26R seating capacity, with their top decks extended completely over the driver's cab. This was the largest seating capacity of any of the seventy SOS REDDs. The final three had MCCW metal-framed bodies to the same design as the original Brush-bodied REDDs and looked like a lowbridge equivalent to Midland Red's HA 8041–8050. These were supplied as chassis only and became 244–246 (AVT 564–566), whereas all the other PMT REDDs were supplied complete with Midland Red effectively acting as agents for the operating company. The chassis of the Potteries REDDs was totally standard and they were exactly the same as those REDDs supplied to Midland Red two years earlier. All the three batches of REDDs supplied to PMT weighed about 6.25 tons and therefore, with a good power-to-weight ratio, had a distinctly sprightly performance but in only obtaining about 7 mpg from their 6.373 litre petrol engines, they were at an immediate disadvantage when compared to the contemporary Leyland 'Titan' TD3 fitted with an oil engine.

One of the Midland Red REDDs, HA 8002, was immediately sold to Northern General and was fitted with an oil engine and subsequently rebodied in 1945 with a Northern Coachbuilders H30/25R body in 1945.

BMMO

1398 (HA 8031) (Above)

The deep-domed roof distinguished the BMMO SOS REDDs with Brush bodies from the first four lowbridge PMT vehicles of 1932. The exaggerated semi-piano-front of these Brush-bodied buses rather spoilt the rest of what was a fairly modern-looking double-decker. There were fifteen Brush-bodied REDDs which were of composite construction, i.e. wooden-framed but with metal strengthening gussets where vertical and horizontal frames were joined together. This official photograph of 1398 (HA 8031), taken in October 1932, suggests that the deep head-clearance in the upper saloon rather made up the highbridge nature of this H26/26R bodywork as the proportions of the rest of the bodywork look remarkably similar to their Brush-bodied cousins. (Brush)

1380 (HA 8005) (Opposite top)

By 1947 the remnants of long-abandoned tram tracks are only just visible in Oldbury Road as one of the Midland Red's rather strange-looking SOS REDDs speeds past the entrance of the former West Smethwick tram depot. These 1932-built buses were the first modern double-deckers to be operated by BMMO. The narrow cab and the oddly-shaped front upper saloon panel rather spoilt the looks of the fifty-two-seat body built by Short Brothers. This style of piano-front was not replicated on the Short-bodied PMT SOS REDDs, which had a full length upper deck over the driver's cab, albeit an ungainly looking affair. 1380 (HA8005) is working on the B87 service which replaced the BCT 87 tram route on 30 September 1939. From that date the replacement bus service to Dudley was always operated by Midland Red. (A. N. Porter)

1409 (HA 8043) (Above)

Standing in St Margaret's Bus Station in Leicester is 1409 (HA 8043). This was one of just ten Metro-Cammell metal-framed SOS REDDs constructed for Midland Red in 1932. The thicker corner front window is a typical Metro-Cammell feature of the period while the piano-front style is less pronounced on these bodies than on the other SOS REDDs. The bus is working on the 619 service to Queniborough, a village off the Melton Road to the north of the city. The PMT version of this MCCW body had virtually the same lower deck and had a lowbridge side-gangway layout in the upper saloon. Surprisingly the Midland Red REDDs all had a twenty-six/twenty-six seating split which was the same as their lowbridge PMT counterparts, although by this time 1409 had, like all the Midland Red versions, been up-seated in the upper saloon by three. (D. R. Harvey Collection)

Potteries Motor Traction

27 (VT 8601) (Above)

27 (VT 8601) was the first of the four SOS REDDs delivered in October 1932. These were the first double-deckers in the PMT fleet and revolutionised the carrying capacity and the running time headways on the Burslem to Tunstall and Longton to Hanley services. From the nearside, the lowbridge Brush bodies seemed to be quite well proportioned and were virtually the lowbridge version of the Midland Red Brush-bodied highbridge version. The seating capacity was for twenty-six in each saloon with the bench seats on the upper saloon being very spaciously set out. The somewhat unattractive semi-'piano-front' treatment and the set-back front of the upper deck really belonged to a style of about three years earlier, when front-axle loading weights on double-deckers such as the AEC 'Regent' 661, Dennis 'Lance' and Leyland 'Titan' TD1 and TD2 were very tightly controlled by the contemporary Construction and Use Regulations. (J. Cooke Collection)

29 (VT 8603) (Opposite top)

From the front, the 1932 Brush-bodied SOS REDDs delivered in October of that year to Potteries Motor Traction looked archaic when compared to other contemporary double-deckers. This rather spoilt the appearance of the otherwise modern bodywork, but what the operator specified is what the coach-builder produced! The cab was perhaps not quite as narrow as on previous SOS single-deckers, but with the radiator and engine being slightly offset to the nearside it really was a disappointment that these SOS REDDs could not have accommodated a more modern cab treatment, though it would follow in part with the 1934 deliveries. The eccentric semi-'piano-front' style between the decks was made even more peculiar by the positioning of the single-line destination aperture. All of these first four PMT REDDs survived the Second World War, with 28 lasting until 1949. (J. Cooke Collection)

237 (AVT 557) (Below)

Longton Bus Station in 1944 shows a wide range of pre-war and war-time double-deckers, but the centrepiece of the view is an SOS REDD. 237 (AVT 557) is one of the Short-bodied fifty-six-seaters built in 1934. The twelve Short bodies built for PMT eliminated the semi-piano-front style, as carried by the Leyland 'Titan' TD3 to the left, and in so doing increased the seating capacity of the buses by four in the upper saloon. The whole effect, however, is spoilt by the complete lack of overall design concept. The long front in the upper saloon which should have improved the appearance of these buses looks like an afterthought, while the cab area just does not 'mate-up' with the rest of the lower saloon. All this is coupled to the fitment of smaller-diameter front tyres, which encourages the illusion that the whole front end of the bus is tipping forward! Despite the obvious lack of war-time maintenance, 237 would struggle on until its withdrawal in 1948. (J. Cooke Collection)

245 (AVT 565) (Above)
There were just three Metro-Cammell-bodied SOS REDDs supplied in 1934 and these could
be distinguished by the thicker front corner pillars in the upper saloon. This was because
these bodies were metal-framed. However, if that was a new concept for the Potteries
company, the vestigial piano-front, whilst less pronounced than on the 1932 Brush-bodied
examples, was still evident. The lowbridge MCCW bodywork looked almost like a squashed
version of the same manufacturer's products built for Midland Red. The windscreen on
these later REDDs was much wider and considerably improved the appearance of these
double-deckers, while this extra width made the cab more spacious and comfortable for the
driver. The rest of the lowbridge Metro-Cammell body did have vestiges of the 1933 body
design, being constructed on a variety of chassis for Birmingham Tramways & Omnibus
Department, but even they had rid themselves of the peculiar front 'tween decks. (J. Cull)

241 (AVT 561) etc. (Opposite top)
This line-up of six SOS REDDs shows 241 (AVT 561) on the right with 243 (AVT 563).
These buses were, like all the Potteries vehicles of this type, built to a lowbridge specification.
These two, along with the fourth and sixth vehicles, had Short Brothers bodies and dated
from 1934. These bodies eliminated the piano-front which was most exaggerated on the
Brush bodied vehicles of 1932, two of which are the third and sixth buses from the right.
The longer upper deck on these Rochester-built bodies enabled an extra four passengers to
be accommodated on the top deck, giving an increased seating capacity of L30/26R. The
two Brush-bodied REDDs have kept their pre-war livery with two white bands between
the decks but the Short-bodied ones, seen just after the end of the Second World War, are
painted very drably with poor-quality war-time paint. (J. Cull)

Northern General
593 (HA 8002) (Above)

SOS FEDD HA 8002 was numerically the second of the production batch. It was originally numbered 1374 in the Midland Red fleet. In October 1932, when only a few months old it was demonstrated to Northern General, having apparently never being used. Within a year it was numbered 593. The bus was first fitted with a Short H26/26R body, but in 1945 it was re-engined with an SOS 8.028 litre direct-injection oil engine. At the same time it was rebodied with a brand-new Northern Coach Builders H30/26R body. In this guise 593 survived until 1952, when it was withdrawn and the SOS REDD chassis broken up. The body was subsequently transferred to 1395 (EWL 749), a 1937 AEC 'Regent' 0661 which had been purchased from City of Oxford Motor Services in 1950. It is working on the 21 route to Easington Lane after being rebodied. The only thing to spoil the appearance of the bus was the antiquated original radiator. (D. R. Harvey Collection)

SOS LRR (Low Rolls-Royce)

In 1932, Midland introduced a new thirty-seat coach. This was the LRR type and was based on the REDD type chassis with an underslung worm differential which immediately reduced the overall height of the vehicles, with the saloon area being several inches lower than the cab, which was a narrow affair which tapered towards the front and gave the impression of a greenhouse tacked onto the front of the vehicle. The wheelbase was 17 feet 6 inches and was, when fitted with an attractive, if somewhat quirky Short Brothers body, 27 feet 4.5 inches long. The coaches weighed 5 tons 16 cwt 1 qtr. These coaches had the newly introduced SOS RR2 LB 6.373 litre petrol engine which was coupled to a five-speed crash gearbox. A total of thirty-one SOS LRRs were produced for Midland Red, with a single vehicle going to Potteries Motor Traction.

BMMO

1643 (AHA 588)
The SOS LRR was a luxurious thirty-seat coach and with its double-decker underslung differential, the body was built very low. AHA 588 has just been completed by Short Brothers and is posed by them on the Esplanade overlooking the River Medway at Rochester, Kent. In their pomp, with their five-speed gearboxes, these coaches were as good as anything else being produced by other manufacturers in the mid-1930s. The paintwork on the coach was beautifully detailed in a red, maroon-and-yellow livery lined out in gold. (A. Ingram)

1656 (AHA 601) (Top)
During the Second World War, the SOS LRR coaches were rebuilt as thirty-four-seat buses, but this conversion hardly concealed the luxurious past of these vehicles. The high-set cab was in contrast to the low-build of the passenger area. 1656 (AHA 601) is parked in Herbert Road, Bearwood in about 1947 and has been freshly repainted in the contemporary lined-out all-over red livery. As a bus it had an eleven-year career, not being withdrawn until 1952. (A. N. Porter)

Potteries Motor Traction

247 (AVT 567) (Above)
Potteries 247 was the only SOS LRR coach not to enter service with Midland Red. Registered AVT 567, as with the other LRRs it was fitted with a Short C30F and entered service in 1934. As one of the Midland Red batch of thirty LRRs, this half-cab, low-height coach was identical save for the Potteries name on the radiator header tank. Later numbered 227 in 1935, it survived until 1949 when it was sold to a showman and eventually had its engine and radiator removed. (A. D. Broughall)

SOS ON (Onward)

Midland Red introduced its new SOS ON model in 1934 and was built to the new maximum length of 27 feet 6 inches for two-axle single-deck buses and coaches. This, coupled with the compact SOS RR2 LB, 6.373 litre petrol engine, enabled the bonnet length to be very short which in turn allowed a longer space for the passengers and enabled the capacity to be increased to thirty-eight seats. The bodies built by Short Brothers were 27 feet 5¾ inches long on a wheelbase of 17 feet 6.37 inches.

A total of 131 of the petrol-engined SOS ONs were built between 1934 and 1936. Of these Midland Red received eighty-three ONs, with the Northern General Group receiving twenty-six vehicles in 1934 and Trent Motor Traction getting twenty-two over the three years of production. The last twelve of the Trent ONs, six from 1935 and six from 1936, were fitted with C30F bodies built by Duple. The SOS ON was the last SOS design to be supplied to more than one other member of the BET Group. This was due to the better availability of more oil-engined vehicles being manufactured by AEC, Daimler and Leyland, with their respective 'Regal', COG5 and 'Tiger' TS models. In the case of Northern, the reasons are more complex as under the auspices of their chief engineer, G. W. Hayter, they introduced their own advanced SE6 single-decker, a forty-four-seater with an American Hercules petrol engine fitted under the floor on the offside. The SE6 and its later four-wheel version, the SE4, was manufactured at the company's works in Gateshead and approximately sixty chassis were built. This effectively prevented any further purchases from BMMO of their SOS buses.

BMMO

1515 (HA 9466) (Opposite above)
The Short Brothers B38F body on the SOS ON 1515 (HA 9466) was never rebuilt and was one of the first of the class to be withdrawn in 1952. It had been fitted with a BMMO K type oil engine and re-designated as a CON in 1938. The bodies on these ONs were ordered from Shorts as a block order for Northern, Wakefields and Sunderland District and were therefore virtually the same, though as was normal, the Midland Red examples were not fitted with destination boxes on the front dome. (M. Rooum)

1626 (AHA 521) (Opposite below)
Working on the 586 service to Rugby in about 1955, 1626 (AHA 521) stands in Pool Meadow Bus Station in Coventry. This SOS ON entered service in 1935 but was one of forty-four of the type converted to a CON type (Converted ON) in 1938 by being fitted with the new BMMO 8.028 litre oil engine. There were fifty ONs delivered to Midland Red in 1934–5, all of which had Short Brothers B38F bodies which took advantage of the maximum length for single-deckers of 27 feet 6 inches. By this time the body had been rebuilt by Hooton in 1952 with rubber-mounted saloon windows which, while practical, rather detracted from their original graceful lines. (C. Carter)

1638 (AHA 533) (Above)
Standing on the parking area opposite St Margaret's Bus Station in Leicester is the
unrebuilt SOS ON 1638 (AHA 533). This bus entered service in 1935 and retained its
petrol engine until it was withdrawn in 1952. 1638 still has the lined-out red livery with
a silver roof and retains the waist-rail mouldings below the saloon windows. The porch
entrance took the intending passenger up three steps into the flat saloon where they could
sit in one of the thirty-eight well-upholstered seats, though the single-skinned ceiling and
side-panels were distinctly more spartan. (S. N. J. White)

Northern General
613 (CN 6019) (Opposite top)
The Short bodies built on the 1934 batch of SOS ONs were based on the standard Midland
Red body designs and were fitted with the recently introduced NGT large destination
box. The fuel tanks were fitted in the traditional location between the wheelbase. There
were twelve SOS ONs delivered to Northern General, numbered 609–620. They were all
delivered in April and May of that year and constituted the final SOS vehicles purchased
new by Northern. All of them were requisitioned by the Ministry of Transport for the
War Department in July 1940 but only nine of them were returned to NGT in the autumn
of 1942 or early 1943. 613 (CN 6019) was the only one to be delivered back to an
independent operator, in this case Brookes Brothers of Castle Gresley. (D. R. Harvey
Collection)

617 (CN 6023) (Below)

The nearside of the NGT SOS ON 617 (CN 6023) shows the much neater arrangement with this new chassis. The front design was helped by the heavily radial windscreen and as a further development, the width of the cab was once again increased. All these buses were fitted with the attractive mouldings below the saloon windows. These buses seated thirty-four passengers in quite spacious conditions as the very short engine/cab length on SOS chassis enabled the front bulkhead to be placed well forward. This allowed the passenger-carrying area to be longer, giving greater legroom over contemporary NGT AEC 'Regals'. Seen in about 1939 on a private hire, the bus has the word 'NORTHERN' on the radiator header tank as well as the SOS lettering on the radiator. 617 was requisitioned in July 1940 and was renumbered 1044 on its return to NGT in January 1943. It was rebodied by Pickering in 1947 and with this body survived until 1954. (W. J. Haynes)

1006 (CN 6020) (Above)
Formerly 614, on its return from the War Department this SOS ON was renumbered
1006. In 1947 it was rebodied by Pickering with a B34F body that had traces of the
war-time 'utility' bodies, despite Pickering not building single-deck bodies during the
war. These bodies had the comfortable original seats which rather belied the very square-
set, basic and functional bodies. The Northern General group had developed a strategy
for operating and even building their own lightweight single-deckers, so these Pickering
bodies, which were also built on Albion 'Valkyrie' chassis for the Red & White group,
only followed this policy, with NGT purchasing some seventy of this style of body.
(S. N. J. White)

1043 (CN 6022) (Opposite above)
Seen in pristine condition after rebodying by Pickering of Wishaw in 1947, 1043 (CN
6022) has yet to be fitted with destination blinds and headlights. Looking as good as it
ever would with black beading and lined-out panels, in this condition the angular lines
of the bodies were almost masked. These bodies were very basic, but enabled Northern
General to squeeze some more life out of their ONs, in this case until 1955 when 1043
was finally taken out of service. (Courtesy of Go Ahead Northern)

Sunderland District
133 (UP 8910) (Opposite below)
The final ten SOS buses sold to Sunderland District were numbered 124–133 in the fleet.
They were virtually identical to those supplied to Midland Red, but they were originally
only thirty-two-seaters. The main difference to the SOS ONs supplied to the 'home'
manufacturer was the provision of a neat, if somewhat small, single-line destination
box. The usual SOS positioning of the petrol tank under the back of the driver's cab
meant that the cab door was, as on most contemporary SOS vehicles, located at the

extreme front of the cab, the pair of hinges for the door being visible near to the offside sidelight. Withdrawals began in 1947, but eight managed to survive until 1950. At the end of its career, the final member of the batch, 133 (UP 8910), was looking a little down at heel, not long before its withdrawal in 1951. This bus had been used by Short, the coach-builder, as the vehicle used for the official body-builders photograph in 1934. (D. R. Harvey Collection)

128 (UP 8905) (Above)

The ten Sunderland District ONs were built in 1934 as thirty-two-seaters and were converted to B38F at the beginning of the war. Unlike many of the NGT ONs, these buses were not impressed by the Ministry of Supply. 128 (UP 8905) was the last survivor of the ten Sunderland District SOS ONs, surviving until 1952. At the end of its operational career it was sold for use as a caravan. With boarded-up windows, this last survivor of the batch stands in a farm yard at Fulwell Mill in March 1961. (Courtesy R. Kell)

Trent Motor Traction

684 (RC 1804) (Opposite top)

The bodies on the 1934 batch of Trent SOS ONs were built by Duple of Hendon and this style was known as the 'Rodney' type. The bodies had straight waist-rails which rather belied their luxurious interiors as well as masking the by-now rather dated ON-type front end. Trent classified these dozen deliveries as thirty-two-seat dual-purpose vehicles and they were used on the company's prestigious long-distance stage carriage services. They were fitted with the SOS RR2LB six-cylinder petrol engines and BMMO's silent third crash gearbox. Unlike contemporary Midland Red ONs, these SOS vehicles had the petrol tank in the conventional position on the offside rather than beneath the driver's seat in the cab. 684 (RC 1804) is in Nottingham Bus Station and is on the Derby via Sandiacre service. (D. R. Harvey Collection)

508 (RC 1808) (Above)

The former Duple-bodied dual-purpose SOS ON 688 (RC 1808) was rebodied in 1947 with a stylish four-bay B35F body built by Willowbrook. At the same time these buses were thoroughly overhauled and fitted with AEC 7.57 litre oil engines which effectively reclassified them as DON-types. 688, as it was renumbered in 1949, survived in service until 1955. This bus was initially renumbered 378 and in 1949 was given the fleet number 508. The aluminium extension through which the crankcase starting handle protrudes was just to make the buses look more modern! (S. N. J. White)

630 (RC 2551) (Above)

Trent received six SOS ONs in March 1935, with 630 (RC 2551) being the last of the class. The bodies built on these petrol-engined ONs were genuine coach bodies built with a luxurious C31F layout by Duple. The bodies had the stepped waist-rail that became identified with streamlining during the mid-1930s. Similarly streamlined was the curved roof-line as well as the slightly arched entrance above the sliding door. It is standing in Nottingham in May 1935 awaiting an excursion duty, although these coaches were used on long-distance tours to the Scottish Highlands, North and Mid Wales, the Lake District and to the resorts of the South West. The coaches were destined not to have long lives. Reseated to C35F in 1938, all the coaches saw restricted use during the Second World and were withdrawn in 1946. (G. H. F. Atkins)

631 (RC 3741) (Opposite above)

Weighing in at a creditably light 5 tons 19 cwt, 631 (RC 3741) is seen when new in 1936. The six coaches were several hundredweight lighter than the earlier ON coaches in an attempt to prevent the overheating which dogged the previous 625–630 class. These were the last petrol-engined SOS single-deckers to be delivered to Trent and had Duple C31F bodies which had a somewhat 'stripped-out' specification with flat-topped seats with thinner cushions in an attempt to lighten the previous somewhat portly 1935 batch of coaches. The overall result is rather smart, but by not being converted to oil engines they inevitably had short lives, being withdrawn by 1948. (D. R. Harvey Collection)

633 (RC 3743) (Opposite below)

There were another six SOS ONs with Duple C31F bodies delivered in 1936. The design was slightly modified with a flatter-topped entrance above the sliding door while the saloon windows were slightly less shapely when compared to the Duple-bodied coaches

of the previous year. These coaches were fitted with trafficators and had a new diamond-shaped PMT logo coupled to a streamlined livery of two-tone red body below a white roof. The Duple body design was perpetuated in 1938 when six Daimler COG5/40 coaches were delivered. 633 (RC 3743) is being employed on a south-east coast excursion in pre-war days. (C. W. Routh)

Wakefields

68 (FT 3156)

In 1934, the previously independent Wakefields Motor Service Company was absorbed into the main Tynemouth & District fleet. The fleet numbers of the buses were given either 'T' or 'W' prefixes and it was at this time that Tynemouth/Wakefields purchased their last two BMMO vehicles. These were numbered W68 and W69 and were ON type single-deck chassis which were fitted with Short B38F bodywork. Both were rebodied by Pickering with B34F bodies in 1948 after being requisitioned by the War Department between 1940 and 1943. By now renumbered 1161 in the main Northern General fleet, FT 3156 waits to pick up passengers in about 1950 when its very utilitarian bodywork was about two years old. The bus would remain in service until 1955. (D. R. Harvey Collection)

SOS DON (Diesel Onward)

By the early 1930s bus manufacturing had to respond to the economics of running a bus service at a profit. The petrol engine was barely capable of more than about 7 mpg, whereas the recently developed oil engine was far more economical, giving in excess of over 12 mpg. SOS needed to evolve its own diesel engine and early diesel SOS buses, known as the DON models, had AEC 7.57 litre indirect-injection units. These were six inches longer than the SOS petrol unit and the space lost reduced capacity to thirty-six. Fitted with a crash gearbox, the SOS DONs were fitted with Brush bodies with either thirty-six bus seats or thirty-four dual-purpose seats.

In 1934 and 1935 Midland Red had fifty-two SOS DONs while in 1935 and 1936 Trent Motor Traction received seventy DON chassis, of which thirty chassis had Midland Red-style Brush bodies and the remaining forty were bodied with B36F bodies constructed by Brush but not supplied, as had previously been the case, by BMMO. The last of the DONs with original bodies were withdrawn in 1953, but twenty of the 1936 buses were rebodied by Willowbrook in 1949 with B35F bus bodies.

BMMO
1698 (AHA 583)
The Brush official photograph of 1698 (AHA 583) dates from September 1935. The Midland Red and Trent orders were built by Brush at the same time and all were given BMMO body numbers. Thus body number 2415 went to AHA 583 and Trent's RC 2715 had body number 2434. The generic family resemblance was still obvious but the longer AEC oil engine meant that the bonnet was longer. While the driver enjoyed a more comfortable cab, the rest of the bodywork had to be modified in order to keep within the legal overall length of 27 feet 6 inches. The resulting body alterations meant that the first saloon bay behind the porch entrance was shorter while the entrance itself was a few inches wider. Perhaps more surprisingly for the mid-1930s bus was that the rear wheels were covered with spats when they were new. (Brush)

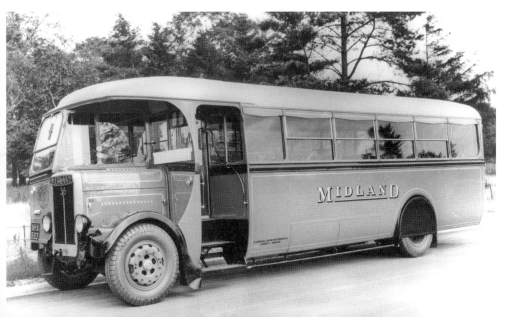

1699 (AHA 584) (Above)
The offside view of one of the SOS DONs shows just how much had to be 'jiggled' about to get the AEC engine into the bus. The window in the cab over the fuel filler was almost twice as long as on the previous SOS ONs, while the first two saloon windows behind the bulkhead were of equal length but were shorter than the remaining saloon windows on this side.

  1699 (AHA 584) waits for its next duty in St Margaret's Bus Station in Leicester before 1950, as that was the year it was renovated by Nudd Brothers and Lockyer, increasing the life of the bus by another five years. (D. R. Harvey Collection)

1711 (AHA 546) (Opposite top)
Most rebuilt single-deck bodies were dealt with by Nudd or Hooton and usually had rubber-mounted saloon windows. However, about twenty DONs were rebuilt at Midland Red's own Carlyle Road Works with new all-metal sides, square-shaped sliding ventilators with only the rear part opening and non-radial saloon windows. 1711 (AHA 546) was one of these rebuilds and although in later years it did look rather minimalistic, when freshly painted and recently rebuilt, these Carlyle renovations had a purposeful, 'no messing about' appearance! It is interesting that some of the DONs owned by Trent were similarly rebuilt, though a complete rebody later became the favoured option. 1711 waits on the parking lot opposite St Margaret's Bus Station in Leicester in about 1949. (D. R. Harvey Collection)

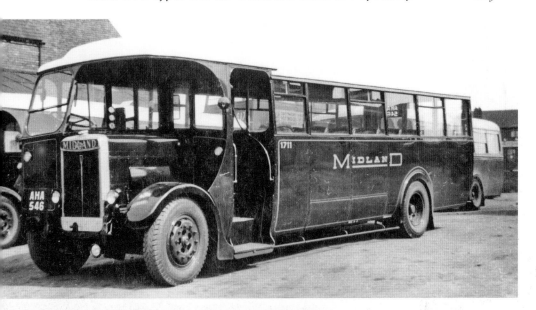

Trent Motor Traction

315 (RC 2715) (Above)

The 1935 deliveries to Trent of SOS DONs consisted of thirty buses bodied by Brush with either thirty-four or thirty-six seats. These DONs were Trent's first diesel-engined buses bought new and were very similar to the Midland Red equivalent ONs (see AHA 583). This is 315 (RC 2715), the first of the fifteen B34F-bodied buses, weighing 5 tons 12 cwt, occupying the second half of the batch. It was delivered to Trent in June 1935. They carried the coach-style pre-war livery and with their reduced seating capacity of two-and-more luxurious seating, were strictly more of a dual-purpose vehicle, being suited to long-distance stage carriage work and excursions. (Brush)

303 (RC 2703) (Above)
After the Second World War, Trent undertook a fairly extensive rebuild of the first thirty Brush-bodied SOS DONs. 303 (RC 2703) shows how the rebuilt buses were modified, giving them a very utilitarian, stripped out look. Gone were the body mouldings, the curved-edge window pans and the glass louvres over the saloon windows. Standing in the Derby Cattle Market in Meadow Road, Derby, the bus would soon be picked up by its crew and taken across the road to the Central Bus Station. (S. N. J. White)

317 (RC 2717) (Opposite top)
Standing alongside a Manchester Corporation MCCW-bodied Leyland 'Titan' PD1/3 in Lower Mosley Street bus station on 20 August 1949 is Trent Road Car 317 (RC 2717). The Brush bodies were similar to those supplied to Midland Red except that they were equipped with destination blinds in the front dome. These buses were the first diesel oil-engined buses in the Trent fleet and were fitted with AEC 7.57 litre engines. This longer engine meant that the saloon on the DONs was shorter, resulting in the reduction of the first saloon bay behind the entrance. (D. Tee)

321 (RC 2721) (Above)
In Trent's Uttoxeter Road garage is the soon-to-be-preserved 321 (RC 2721). This
SOS DON entered service in July 1935. In the mid-1950s Trent operated a year-round
limited-stop service from Derbyshire to Skegness and the coast as well as extra summer
season services that gave many smaller villages a direct service to the seaside resorts on
the Lincolnshire coast. 321 had been converted in 1952 for use at Skegness as a mobile
booking and enquiry office while also being used as a waiting room. The body was rebuilt
with a wider doorway, replacing seats to give more limited capacity and constructing an
enquiry counter. The bus was at first driven back to Derby for the winter season but
eventually it was towed to and from Derby. After 321 was finally withdrawn it passed to
the LVVS in 1962, who continued to use it for many years as their publicity vehicle. After
many years of inactivity, in 2009 a start was made to restore it back to a fully operational
bus. (P. J. Yeomans)

332 (RC 3703) (Above)
The height of pre-war elegance! Trent's 332 (RC 3703), an SOS DON with an AEC oil engine and a Brush B36F body, entered service in April 1936. Adorned with chrome strips and beading, a white roof equipped with advertising slip board proclaiming the Derby Hippodrome Theatre, the bus has also got the shapely, long front wings that were fitted to these Trent vehicles when they were new and an aluminium sheet at the bottom of the radiator, just above the starting handle, fitted in winter in order to encourage the bus to warm up. 332 had been working on one of the many works services to the Rolls-Royce factory in Derby. (C. W. Routh)

354 (RC 3725) (Opposite top)
The second order was delivered in 1936 and there were some major differences to the body design which represented, for the first time, a move away from Midland Red-styled bodywork, even though the coachwork was still manufactured by Brush. The windscreen was taller and was lacking the graceful radial curves of the 1935 deliveries while the rear dome was somewhat squarer and, as in previous deliveries, was graced with a single-line destination box. The buses also broke with the normal SOS tradition by having the fuel tank located on the offside between the wheelbase. The vehicles were again originally painted in the two-tone dual-purpose livery while the fuel tank was located between the wheelbase on the offside. (Lens of Sutton)

368 (RC 3739) (Above)

About to pick up passengers in Derby's Central Bus Station just after the Second World War is 368 (RC 3739). This second batch of AEC oil-engined SOS DONs were delivered in 1936 as 330 to 369 in the Trent fleet. It is working on the 31 route to Uttoxeter via Ashbourne and Rocester. This was classified as a direct service and during the war had been numbered as the 33 route. 368 was one of eighteen of the class not to be rebodied by Willowbrook in 1949 and as a result 368 was, as were all the unrebodied buses, withdrawn by 1952. (A. Ingram)

517 (RC 3712) (Above)
Twenty of the 1936 batch of SOS DONs were rebodied in 1949 by Willowbrook with
attractively deep-windowed B35F bodywork and were renumbered 512–531. These
followed on from the similarly rebodied SOS ONs of 1934 which had been renumbered
501–511. This Willowbrook body design was also fitted to some sixteen 1938 AEC
'Regal' 0662 buses in 1950. 517 (RC 3712) is parked on the coach park in Skegness,
showing that when first rebodied, these buses were regarded as dual-purpose vehicles and
as such were capable of use as day excursion vehicles. (W. J. Haynes)

530 (RC 3737) (Opposite top)
Setting down its passengers outside the Barton information hut in the Huntingdon
Street Bus Station in Nottingham is 530 (RC 3737). This was one of the 1936 SOS
DONs, originally with a Brush body, that was rebodied by Willowbrook with a B35F
body in 1949. This style of body was also fitted in the following year to sixteen AEC
'Regal' 0662s whose chassis were one year newer than the DONs. 530 was originally
numbered 366, but the twenty rebodied 1936 DONs were renumbered as a block from
512–531. (R. H. G. Simpson)

363 (RC 3734) (Above)

One of the SOS DONs, 363 (RC 3734) was converted to a dual-control trainer in 1952 and given a full front in order to accommodate the instructor's controls. The bus was renumbered 22, replacing the previous dual-control trainer numbered 15 from a former Midland Red SOS FS which had been acquired in 1935 and operated until 1952. As 22, this DON was kept in service until the 1960s. It is standing in Derby Bus Station when waiting for its trainee driver to turn up to take his lesson. (P. J. Yeomans)

357 (RC 3728)
Just like their Midland Red cousins, many of the SOS DONs led an interesting afterlife as showmen's vehicles. Trent 357 (RC 3728) was one of the Brush thirty-six seaters delivered to Trent in April 1936. It was not one of the twenty of the batch chosen to be rebodied by Willowbrook in 1949 and was subsequently withdrawn early in September 1951. Like many an SOS, it turned up with a showman, in this case one based in Coventry, with whom it survived until 1959. Unlike many SOS bues that finished their lives with showmen on the fairground circuit, RC 3728 appears to have been used as an accommodation vehicle, that is a lived-in mobile caravan. If the body was made watertight, in this condition, an SOS chassis could last well into its second decade as a mobile caravan, following the fairgrounds around the Midlands and providing a comfortable home for the barkers, stallholders and ride owners. (A. D. Broughall)

1004 (RC 3326) (Opposite)
One of Trent Motor Traction's SOS FEDDs, 1004 (RC 3326) is painted in the early post-war livery, which makes an interesting comparison with the tmuch more numerous Midland Red equivalents. It is leaving Mount Street Bus Station in Nottingham en route to Derby and is positively groaning under its full complement of passengers. The substitution of an AEC 7.57 litre diesel engine in 1943 instead of the original 8 litre petrol unit would have improved the fuel economy but made the performance a little less lively. The sliding front entrance doors could prove something of a mixed blessing on both the Trent and Midland Red FEDDs, either sliding back and forth under the acceleration of deceleration of the bus, or jamming on its runners. It appears, however, that the doors on 1004 are locked in the open position, revealing the TRENT fleet nameplate on the entrance step riser, as if to remind passengers on whose bus they were riding! The bus is carrying an advertisement for Burrows & Sturgess, who were established in 1850 and who made soft drinks in various locations in Derby until the late 1960s. (R. Marshall)

SOS FEDD (Front-Entrance Double-Decker)

The REDD model was superseded after the construction of a prototype in 1933 by the SOS FEDD. This front-entrance double-decker went into production in 1934 and by the autumn of 1939 some 350 of these impressive buses were built, of which Trent Motor Traction received fifteen intended for Midland Red. In 1934 Midland Red received fifty Short Brothers FEDDs and from the 1938 orders all the Midland Red FEDDs had composite Brush H30/26F bodies.

It was from the 1935–36 order that SOS FEDDs were sold to another BET company. The Midland Red order to be delivered in 1936 was for 150 FEDDs, although two vehicles, 1743 and 1744, were delivered in December 1935. The mechanical specification of the new double-decker bus was very similar to the previous REDD design. It had the SOS RR2 LB six-cylinder side-valve petrol engine of 6.373 litres and a 'silent third' gearbox, with a wheelbase of 16 feet 3¼ inches. The body contract was placed with Metro-Cammell, but unlike the previous orders for FEDDs, the bodies were metal-framed. They had an H30/26R seating capacity and superficially looked like the fifty earlier Short-bodied FEDDs supplied to Midland Red in 1934, having the attractive curve above the driver's cab. Having metal-framed bodies, the Metro-Cammell FEDDs weighed 6 tons 14 cwt, ensuring a durability that meant that none of these buses required major rebuilding during their long lives.

The way in which the buses were delivered was a little complex because Trent Motor Traction, who had purchased some ninety-four SOS ON and DON single-deckers between 1934 and 1936, were short of double-deckers. The chassis numbers of these buses were in the 2134 to 2233 range, with 2141/51/61–62/68–71/73–79 going to Trent. As a result, fifteen of the first order of 100 MCCW-bodied SOS FEDDs for Midland Red were transferred to Trent, which was a fellow BET company. These buses took the Trent fleet numbers 1000–1014 (RC 3322-3336) and were the only SOS double-deckers purchased by the company. One FEDD, 1002, was lost in a fire in 1948 but all the others were withdrawn between 1950 and 1951, which was around three years earlier than the Midland FEDDs.

BMMO

1746 (BHA 305)

During May 1952, Stan Laurel and Oliver Hardy, as part of their British tour, were starring at the Birmingham Hippodrome, featured on the billboard advertisement above the railway bridge parapet behind 1746 (BHA 305). This 1936-built bus entered service in January 1936 and was one of the first 100 of the metal-framed MCCW SOS FEDDs. It is painted in the fully lined-out post-war livery with a silver roof. Although re-engined with a BMMO K type oil engine in 1944, the bus was largely unaltered throughout its nineteen-year operational life, a testimony to the excellent construction of the Metro-Cammell body. The bus is working on the 130 service to Stourbridge via the then fearsome Mucklow Hill and Halesowen. (S. N. J. White)

1837 (BHA 396)

Parked outside Solihull Church in the late 1930s, when working on the 154 service back to Birmingham, is an almost-new Metro-Cammell-bodied SOS FEDD. It is resplendent in its full twin cream bands and silver-roofed livery. Forward-entrance double-deckers were developed in the mid-1930s with the idea, much like today, that the conductor could control the passenger movements, while the option of having a doored entrance appeared to be a real boon, especially in winter. Unfortunately the front entrance frequently led to problems with the body around the front bulkhead but these MCCW-bodied FEDDs were so well constructed that they didn't seem to have this structural weakness. BHA 396 was one of the fifteen BHA 3xx FEDDs that took the numbers of the buses sent to Trent. (J. Cull)

1865 (BHA 824) (Above)

A post-war view of 1865 (BHA 824) standing in Dudley Bus Station when working on one of the intensive services through the Black Country to Cradley Heath. Weighing around 6 tons 14 cwt the only visible problem with the bus is the slightly misaligned sliding door, which was either deliberately wedged open by the conductor to prevent it sliding shut with a body-shaking slam when the bus braked, or had conspired to jam itself open. 1865 received a BMMO oil engine in 1944 while about the same time receiving the modified ventilator on the bonnet side. 1865 was one of the last three BHA-registered FEDDs to survive, not being withdrawn until 1957. (D. R. Harvey Collection)

Trent Motor Traction

1005 (RC 3327) (Opposite top)

An official Metro-Cammell photograph of 1005 (RC 3327) taken in 1936 shows that the Trent SOS FEDDs buses were exactly the same as the Midland Red examples, except that the normal all-over red was given added dark-red livery bands. The fifteen Trent FEDDs had BMMO body numbers 2535–2549 and were originally intended as the last fifteen of the first 100 of the Midland Red vehicles. In the event the Midland Red order was reduced to 135. When they entered service, the fifteen Trent SOS FEDDs were fitted with the SOS RR2LB 6.373 litre petrol engine. They had the 'silent third' gearbox, which was very driver-friendly but coupled with the engine, left these double-deckers somewhat underpowered. In 1943 they all were re-engined with AEC 7.57 litre oil engines, but their strongly built bodies remained in an unrebuilt state until their withdrawal between 1950 and 1951. (Metro-Cammell)

1012 (RC 3334) (Above)

Waiting in the bus station in Derby in about 1937 is one of Trent Motor Traction's SOS FEDDs. The fifteen buses which made up the batch were fitted with Metro-Cammell metal-framed bodies; these double-deckers were fifty-six-seaters with thirty upstairs and twenty-six in the lower saloon. The bus would have been registered in the BHA 3xx series had it not been diverted to Trent, who had a tradition of buying buses from BMMO and were short of double-deckers. 1012 (RC 3334) is fully lined out with thin gold lines and still has the patina of its original coach-builder's paintwork. 1012 is on the route to Alfreton, which is displayed on a roller destination blind, though the barely legible number 1 route number is carried on a stencil. (C. W. Routh)

1013 (RC 3335) (Above)

1013 (RC 3335) is parked in Huntingdon Street Bus Station in Nottingham. It has been painted in the early post-war livery of red and ivory, which on a misty day in the East Midlands would have brightened up the urban landscape. This was one of the fifteen SOS FEDDs built in 1936 with fifty-six seat, forward entrance bodies built by Metro-Cammell. These buses were intended to be part of a batch for Midland Red but were diverted to Trent, who required a quick delivery of new buses. The metal-framed bodies were quite robust, but they were not as long-lived as their Midland Red counterparts, possibly due to their extensive use on the intensive service between Derby and Nottingham, mostly going in 1950 and 1951. Although there were no more FEDDs, the fairly unusual use of forward entrances became the norm for the last of Trent's pre-war double-deckers, although, again somewhat unusually for a BET-owned company, these were on Daimler COG5 chassis. (D. R. Harvey Collection)

1006 (RC 3328) (Opposite top)

The FEDDs were the first new double-deckers supplied to Trent for over two years but the last to be of the SOS marque. Working on one of the variations of the 15 service to Mickleover is Trent's 1006 (RC 3328). It is standing in Derby Bus Station in July 1950 in the last livery version it carried prior to withdrawal. A certain amount of superficial rebuilding has taken place as only the half-drop opening windows have retained their rain louvres. The small war-time headlights fit uncomfortably in the much larger original headlight recesses while the lower body panels are looking somewhat battered, suggesting that 1006 is approaching the end of its working life. (D. Tee)

1011 (RC 3333) (Above)

Awaiting disposal in Derby on 29 April 1951 is a quartet of Trent Metro-Cammell-bodied SOS FEDDs. Although the subsequent double-deckers delivered in 1937 had AEC 'Regent' 661 chassis and those of 1938 and 1939 had Daimler COG5 chassis, the forward-entrance style with a sliding door was perpetuated as the immediate pre-war company standard type. The nearest FEDD is 1011 (RC 3333), which was 'the one that got away' as it survived at the ill-fated Plumtree Museum until 1974, when its body was tipped off the chassis a matter of hours before a team of preservationists came to rescue it! The bus on the left is 1009 (RC 3331), which is also in the later ivory-and-red livery. This contrasts with the double-decker on the right, which is in the early post-war all-over red Trent colour scheme. (D. R. Harvey Collection)

SOS ONC (Onward Coach)

The final type of BMMO coach to be built before the Second World War was the ONC, in a batch of thirty-one. They only differed from the SON bus by having the ZF Aphon four-speed gearboxes with overdrive. Midland Red received twenty-four ONCs and one LON (Luxury ON) in 1939 and all were fitted with full-fronted thirty-seat centre-exit bodies built by Duple. These followed on the design of the 1937 SOS SLR coaches, none of which were ever supplied to any other operator. The SLR bodies had been constructed by English Electric, but the Duple bodies eliminated the stepped waist-rail.

Just six other ONCs were built and again it was Trent Motor Traction who received them. Unlike the Midland Red examples, these had attractive half-cab bodies built by Willowbrook with a C31F layout.

BMMO

2274 (FHA 406)
The Midland Red SOS ONCs had thirty-seat coach bodies built by Duple which were a streamlined development of the previous fifty English Electric-bodied SOS SLR coaches supplied only to Midland Red. They were built with full fronts and really looked a well-proportioned luxury vehicle. 2274 (FHA 406) is being employed on a 'coach cruise' to the Glamorganshire coastal resorts and is parked at Barry Island. The Midland Red ONCs had a curved waist-rail and a minimum of chrome trim, streamlined wings and a central entrance and were the height of refinement. (S. N. J. White)

2277 (FHA 409)
Parked on a rainy day at the Rigby Road coach park in Blackpool is 2277 (FHA 409).
The coach is working on the service to Kidderminster, which left Blackpool at 3:30 p.m.
and would make the first of its drop-offs some five and a half hours later at Quatford.
The Duple bodies had an emergency exit in the middle of the offside, directly opposite the
main sliding entrance door. The Midland Red ONCs had four-speed overdrive gearboxes
which, coupled to the 8.028 litre oil engine, gave a speedy yet comfortable ride. They were
directly related to the SOS SONs, having their overhead worm-drive rear axles rather
than the lower double-decker type found in previous SOS coaches. (H. W. Peers)

2279 (FHA 411) (Above)
Midland Red's day tours were very popular, and from Birmingham – in the days before motorways and with its central England location – only a few seaside resorts could be reached on these outings. Blackpool was a well-liked destination, while Weston-Super-Mare and the North Somerset coast were easily accessible but were timetabled to take five hours. The North Wales coastal resorts were enjoyed but these were, with the often difficult access from England taking five hours and ten minutes, just about possible in one day. 2279 (FHA 411) has made the journey to Rhyl in the company of a post-war BMMO C1 coach. Unlike their Trent counterparts, the Midland Red ONCs had the fuel-filler cap on the nearside in front of the nearside cab door. (S. N. J. White)

2291 (FHA 423) (Opposite top)
Even at the end of their careers, the Midland Red SOS ONCs were still used in front-line duties. In 1959, 2291 (FHA 423) leaves Digbeth Coach Station in Birmingham on an excursion to Bournemouth. This was a real hike, with twenty-minute refreshment stops at Oxford, Newbury and Winchester and a journey time of just over nine and a half hours. By now painted with a black roof, even at twenty years old they carried their age remarkably well. (J. C. Cockshott)

Trent Motor Traction

643 (RC 7083) (Above)

The 1939 SOS ONC coaches for Trent were a very different animal to their Midland Red counterparts. The most obvious difference was that they were half-cab vehicles and had the latest type of polished AEC-style exposed radiator. Their Willowbrook front-entrance bodies, albeit attractive, were of the same somewhat dated style as the 1936 deliveries. With their hipped waist-rails, the six coaches were thirty-one-seaters. The Trent ONCs were fitted with the standard 8.028 litre oil engine and a six-speed gearbox. 643 (RC7083) was the first of the six Trent ONCs. (D. R. Harvey Collection)

644 (RC 7084) (Above)

644 (RC 7084) had its Willowbrook C31F body refurbished and repainted in all-over ivory with a cherry-red painted roof and side flashes, as well as a Gothic-styled fleet name. After being refurbished, the coach was used from 1949 as the Derbyshire County Cricket Club's team coach with a reduced seating capacity of twenty-seven. Despite their luxury, the coaches reverted to having their fuel tanks located in the cab, resulting in the cab door being located about as awkwardly as it was possible to get, with the bottom of the door being placed above the highest point of the offside mudguard. All six Trent ONCs were withdrawn in 1954. (P. J. Yeomans)

646 (RC 7086) (Opposite above)

Loading up with passengers in Cheltenham Coach Station, with an early post-war Bedford OB behind it, is Trent SOS ONC 646 (RC 7086). The coach is working on an Associated Motorways service, though it is not possible to ascertain if the coach is going to or coming from the south-west. With their overdrive gearboxes, the ONCs were well suited to such long-distance excursion work, giving them a good turn of speed and excellent fuel economy. This is one of the reasons why these buses survived so long in front-line service. (D. R. Harvey Collection)

647 (RC 7087) (Opposite below)

Trent had regular summer excursions to the east coast, including to the Lincolnshire resort of Skegness. Already half-full with passengers, 647 (RC 7087) waits in Nottingham in 1947, still in its pre-war livery. These SOS ONCs had a wider windscreen, but the stepped waist-rail with the last three saloon-side windows raised at a different angle belonged to a style developed in the mid-1930s and even when new looked somewhat dated. After repainting in the predominantly cream livery, 647 was operated until 1954 when it was replaced by underfloor-engined Leyland 'Royal Tigers' coaches with Willowbrook bodies. (R. Marshall)

SOS SON (Saloon Onward)

The production SOS SON was a natural development of the ON and DON models. The SON was fitted with the BMMO K type 8.028 litre direct-injection oil engine which was coupled to a four-speed 'silent third' gearbox. Midland Red's first examples were bodied by English Electric while the last two batches for the company received Brush bodies, albeit of two distinct styles. All the Midland Red SONs had a B38F layout. A total of 254 SOS SONs were built for Midland Red but despite its success with its home operator, elsewhere only Trent Motor Traction bought any SONs, with their twenty-six making a grand total of 280 of this model, the last half-cab single-decker SOS type to be constructed.

The Trent Motor Company bought two batches of SON buses, with twelve being delivered in 1939 and fourteen in 1940, the latter being the very last SOSs built. Unlike their Midland Red counterparts, the Trent examples received Willowbrook B34F bodies.

BMMO

2312 (FHA 467) (Opposite above)

The Brush coach-building company based in Loughborough always took official photographs of their buses. One of the last taken, just before the outbreak of the Second World War, was of FHA 467 and was taken in August 1939. The thirty-eight penultimate SOS SONs for Midland Red had a body style that was the last with the vertical rear end developed in 1934 with the ONs, but with a marginally wider windscreen and the latest type of radiator, the idiosyncratic nature of the Midland Red marque had largely been eliminated. The livery of lined-out red with a maroon stripe below the saloon windows, black wings and white roof also softened these high-capacity thirty-eight-seater single-deckers. (Brush)

2317 (FHA 472) (Opposite below)

Within weeks of entering service, the 1939 deliveries of SOS SONs were painted with white blackout wing edges and masked headlights. 2317 (FHA 472) stands alongside Nottingham Victoria Station early in August 1940 and is in the full pre-war livery. On the front dome is the vestige of a front destination box which was never in the body specification laid down by Midland Red. The bus is clearly carrying the black bonnet number 472, which in 1944 would be replaced by the private identification number 2317. This bus would remain in service until 1958, though it was renovated by Nudd Brothers & Lockyer in 1950. (G. H. F. Atkins, courtesy J. Banks)

2305 (FHA 460) (Above)
Picking up passengers near to the Midland Red garage in Cleveland Road, Wolverhampton, is one of the Nudd Brothers & Lockyer-rebuilt Brush-bodied SOS SONs of 1939. The rebuilding of 2305 (FHA 460) meant that the bodywork lost all its side mouldings and the saloon windows were mounted in rubber, *à la une caravane*, which was at odds with the unaltered cab. However, despite a certain amount of waist-rail sag, the rebuilding of these buses extended their life by about seven or eight years. (S. N. J. White)

2415 (GHA 334) (Opposite top)
Despite the outbreak of war, it was still possible to hire a bus for an excursion until the retreat of the BEF from Dunkirk. Parked outside the 'Plough Hotel' in Quedgeley, Gloucestershire, on 26 May 1940 – the day the evacuation began – is GHA 334, which had only been delivered earlier in the same month. These were the last fifty SONs delivered to Midland Red and were also the last SOS-badged buses in the fleet as after Mr L. G. Wyndham Shire retired, his successor Mr Donald Sinclair changed the chassis name from SOS to BMMO. The new style of Brush body was more curvaceous, with a rounded rear end and a deep roof which arguably looked more modern than the Trent SOS SONs that had Willowbrook bodies. The bus was taking RAF personnel, including the photographer, Leslie Perkins back to RAF Quedgeley and so this was the farewell photograph and drink together for some time. Standing by the front wheel of the bus is the wife of the photographer, Mrs Winnie Perkins, and her son Ray. (L. W. Perkins)

2426 (GHA345) (Above)
About a year before it was rebuilt by Nudd Brothers & Lockyer in 1950, 2426 (GHA345) shows off the shapely lines of the Brush body. The bus was delivered in July 1940 and with a seating capacity of thirty-eight was worthy of continuing in service until 1958. This was despite having competition from the post-war underfloor-engined BMMO S6, S8 to S12 single-deckers. The SOS SON body was equipped with used ticket boxes, the first time they had been fitted with this feature. (D. R. Harvey Collection)

2431 (GHA 350) (Above)
Standing in Jamaica Row in Birmingham city centre is the last of the fifty 1940s SOS
SONs, 2431 (GHA 350). The bus has been rebuilt by Nudd Brothers & Lockyer in 1950
with virtually a new body behind the front bulkhead. The six-bay construction bodywork
contained thirty-eight curve-topped seats which were surprisingly comfortable for a stage
carriage vehicle. The short length of the bonnet helped enormously to increase the seating
capacity of the SOS SON model and the Trent vehicles were of a similar style, enabling
them to have well-spaced seating with more legroom, rather than the thirty-eight in the
Midland Red buses. By this date the SOS radiator badge had been replaced by a BMMO
one. (D. R. Harvey Collection)

2418 (GHA 337) (Opposite top)
On the centenary of the formation of the Birmingham & Midland Motor Omnibus
Company, a celebration was held at the Black Country Living Museum in Dudley on 26
November 2004. BaMMOT sent their beautifully preserved SOS SON 2418 (GHA 337).
Entering service in June 1940, the bus was rebuilt in 1950 by Nudd Brothers & Lockyer
with rubber-mounted saloon windows and sliding ventilators and in an all-over red
livery, in which scheme it has been restored. This Midland Red SON makes an interesting
contrast to Trent's slightly later Willowbrook-bodied 417 (RC 7927). (D. R. Harvey)

Trent Motor Traction

409 (RC 7098) (Above)

In original condition with the diamond TMT fleet name introduced in 1936 is SOS SON 409 (RC 7098). There were twelve SOS SONs delivered during 1939, and for the first time they were fitted with the BMMO K type diesel engine rather than the AEC engines fitted to the earlier DONs. These buses had a German-built ZF gearbox which had a 'silent third' ratio which virtually produced a gear-change as smooth as a synchromesh gearbox. The bodywork was built by Willowbrook, who were also based in Loughborough, but their products built on the SOS SON chassis did look shorter and taller due in part to having one less saloon window bay. These bodies had a B34F layout and, as was usual with the SOS-built buses, had the emergency exit as a central door at the rear of the body. These were the first bus, rather than coach bodies built on SOS chassis by the Loughborough-based coach-builder and were less fussy than the previous Brush-bodied examples. (W. J. Haynes)

407 (RC 7096) (Above)
The offside of 1939-built Willowbrook-bodied 407 (RC 7096) makes an interesting comparison with 416 (RC 7926), one of the fourteen SOS SONs of 1940. The older bus shows that the traditional location of the fuel tank, marked by the filler cap, was retained underneath the driver's seat, while 416 had the fuel tank between the wheelbase at chassis level. 407's cab door was at the extreme front of the cab whereas the cab door on the newer vehicle is in the more usual position. It is also noticeable that the framing of the Willowbrook bodies was in pairs, with more slender second, fourth and sixth pillars. Both buses are standing in the Lower Mosley Street Bus Station in Manchester in 1949. (D. Tee)

404 (RC 7093) (Opposite top)
After the Second World War, the Willowbrook bodies of the 1939 batch were overhauled, with the removal of waist-rail mouldings and the streamlined curved livery giving them a more basic appearance. This rebuild, coupled with the later lighter red-and-white post-war livery certainly modernised the appearance of these buses. It was perhaps surprising that the bodies retained all their glass rain shields. 404 (RC 7093) stands in the old Derby Cattle Market in the early 1950s. (S. N. J. White)

421 (RC 7931) (Above)

The second group of Willowbrook-bodied B34F buses built in 1940 were numbered 412–425 in the Trent fleet. These buses were originally presented with the raised TMT diamond-shaped fleet name. 421 (RC 7931) is parked just in front of 419 (RC 7929), a further member of the same class of the last SOS buses constructed for another operator. Despite these buses being constructed after the outbreak of war, they retained all the equipment and features of a pre-war vehicle, including having a curved 'tumblehome' at the bottom of the saloon panelling. The buses also reverted to having the fuel tank located on the offside of the main chassis member. The five brackets on the cantrail were used to support destination slip boards. (D. R. Harvey Collection)

415 (RC 7925) (Above)
The nearside of the SOS SONs with Willowbrook bodies reveals almost for the first (and last) time just how the appearance of these half-cab single-deckers had been enhanced. The saloon windows on the Trent SONs were deeper than on the Brush vehicles previously supplied, which considerably modernised the appearance of these last SOS SON front-engined buses to be constructed at Carlyle Road Works in Birmingham. The modern, stylish radiator with the letters 'TMT' on the header tank was a great improvement on the mid-1930s style, and the much wider windscreen and cab modernised the appearance of these buses enormously. 415 (RC 7925) is seen in the years immediately after the war and is still in its original attractive livery style. (S. N. J. White)

414 (RC 7924) (Opposite above)
Working on the 21 service to Ashby is 414 (RC 7924). The bus is already loading up with passengers as it stands in Derby Bus Station in the late 1940s and is wearing the lighter red-and-cream livery with the large 'TRENT' fleet name. If there was a design fault in the Willowbrook body design in the welcome inclusion of a destination box, it was that it was very small and did not include the route number. These last SOS SONs remained in service until 1954, which for a BET company was a creditable lifespan. (P. J. Yeomans)

425 (RC 7935) (Opposite below)
This is how many an SOS bus finished up! 425 (RC 7935), a Willowbrook-bodied SON of 1940, is being used as a showman's caravan at a Skipton fairground in July 1962 when still largely in its as-withdrawn condition. The bus has been fitted with a roof-mounted canvas-covered storage area, but the body is otherwise intact, although the porch entrance has been replaced by a wooden door; to gain entrance would have been difficult as the bottom of the home-made door is only at saloon floor level. (C. W. Routh)

417 (RC 7927)

At the Aston Manor Museum in Witton, Birmingham on 11 July 2010 is the preserved 417 (RC 7927). Saved for posterity by the erstwhile Trent Company itself, the single-decker is a fine example of the final flourishing of the front-entrance SOS marque. The Willowbrook body is largely new, but shows how the latter-day Trent specification had moved away from the bodies built by Brush for the Midland Red's own use. Beautifully preserved, this SON comfortably copes with twenty-first century traffic while a ride on this vehicle is both comfortable and quite luxurious, despite it being only a service bus, and it is a fine representative of a surviving pre-war BMMO-built SOS chassis. (D. R. Harvey)

The Post-War Dabble

1957	DEMO TO	S. WALES	NGT	M & D	PMT	W. WE
S15	50	4644	4645	4646	4648	4649

BMMO decided to produce a dual-purpose version of their advanced integral lightweight S14 bus, which had been in production since 1954. Fifty S15s entered service in 1957 with fleet numbers 4601–4650 (601–650 AHA). The buses were fitted with the standard horizontal BMMO 8.028 litre coupled to a four-speed constant-mesh gearbox and had high-ratio back axles and twin sets of rear tyres. The standard coach livery of red with a black roof was adopted, with the two colours being separated by a polished aluminium moulding below the saloon windows, with two short styling strips behind the entrance door on the nearside linking the deep driver's-side cab window with the higher saloon windows. Also, there was a thin polished strip on the guttering above the saloon windows. At the front it also had a neatly shaped, half-sized, vertical-barred radiator grill and a deep windscreen and driver's signalling window, which gave a much neater and somehow more purposeful look when compared to the previous S14 bus body. Much of the bodywork was made of glass fibre, including the front and rear domes and surprisingly the electrically operated front doors.

These Carlyle-bodied dual-purpose vehicles were framed by Metal Section of Oldbury and when fitted out had a capacity of forty passengers, seated in comfortable Dunlopillo bucket seats with cheerful and bright fabric cushions and backrests. The interior colour scheme was a white or yellow ceiling, buff window panels and peony-red side-panels. Each of the six side windows was fitted with pull-in hopper ventilators, but surprisingly the saloon was illuminated by exposed light bulbs. The saloon had, like all post-war S type underfloor engined single-deckers, a wide full-length parcel rack above the side windows at cantrail level.

By 1956, the standard BET Federation single-decker was either an AEC 'Reliance' MU type with an AEC AH470 7.58-litre engine or a Leyland 'Tiger Cub' PSUC1 series with a Leyland 0.350 engine of 5.76 litres still using either constant-mesh or synchromesh gearboxes, although semi-automatic gearboxes were becoming available. There was a move within the BET Group to source single-deckers from other manufacturers such as Albion with their 'Aberdonian' and Guy Motors with their 'Arab' LUF. As a result of trying to cast their net wider, BMMO with their new S15 model were invited to demonstrate to various BET operators. Perhaps the unavailability of the successful, fairly straight forward Bristol LS and MW underfloor-engined single-deckers which were being supplied to the nationalised BTC operators rankled with both the BET management and certain of the BET companies; could there be simple alternative to these AEC and Leyland options? The demonstrations were probably an attempt by the BET group to try and cut unit costs, and BMMO had good connections with parts manufacturers from whom they sourced engine blocks, chassis frames and every component necessary in order to create a bus. Whatever the reasons, five new S15s were sent out around the country in 1957 as demonstrators and were well received by the operators who received them, briefly being considered as a possible alternative to the contemporary BET orders. Although they never received a demonstrator, in 1957 East Midlands MS expressed an interest in purchasing ten BMMO S15s, but the order was altered to ten Willowbrook-bodied Leyland 'Tiger Cub' PSUC1/2s, delivered in 1958.

4644 was demonstrated to South Wales, 4645 went to Northern General and 4646 was tried out by Maidstone and District in the autumn in 1957. Potteries Motor Traction ran 4648 from November 1957 to 7 January 1958 while Western Welsh operated 4649. But for Midland Red's lack of manufacturing capacity, these well-proportioned semi-coaches *might* have become a standard option for the BET group, with BMMO chassis, emulating the 1,000 pre-war SOS buses supplied around the country in the 1920s and 1930s.

If the Northern Group had still been managed by G. W. Hayter there would have been a sort of perfect symmetry if they had purchased the S15 from Midland Red, as the general manager was Donald Sinclair, who had been Hayter's deputy at Gateshead. Sinclair had brought the ideas of the NGT SE4 to Edgbaston and developed the ideas in the rebuilding of the pre-war rear-engined single-deckers to an underfloor-engined layout, ultimately leading to the very successful S types, of which the S15 was by 1957 the latest of this long line.

Alas, it never happened!

4645 (645 AHA) (Opposite above)
Passing through the village of Grindon, County Durham on its way to Consett is 4645 (AHA 645). This BMMO S15 was demonstrated to Northern General in 1957, where it would have been welcomed as it had only been a few years previously that SOS ONs were still being operated. The dual-purpose bus is being used on the long 15 route, where its comfortable seats would have been welcome. (Bristol VBG)

4646 (646 AHA) (Opposite below)
Parked in the Maidstone garage of Maidstone & District on 27 October 1957 is BMMO S15 4646 (646 AHA). The dual-purpose vehicle is being used as a demonstrator to the large Kent-based operator and was operated by them from 10 October until 23 November 1957 on an extended trial which, although reasonably successful, did not result in any orders. It should also be remembered that around the same time Maidstone & District had single-deck demonstrators from Albion and Guy Motors and these visits did not result in any orders either. It is perhaps a little surprising that it didn't put in an appearance as well with the neighbouring East Kent Company. (B. W. Ware)

Conclusion

It would be appropriate to place the history of Midland Red's entry into the open market from 1924 until the outbreak of the Second World War into some sort of context. The Birmingham & Midland Omnibus Company was growing rapidly from the beginning of the 1920s and therefore was sufficiently large as an operator to dictate what type of buses it wished to operate. Their expansion was ruthless, especially in their home area in the West Midlands, where they competed with tramcar services and independent bus operators.

The BMMO requirement was for an easy-to-drive, speedy, economical, lightweight single-decker with a maximum seating capacity. Which operator wouldn't want buses with those criteria? Contemporary buses were large, lorry-like and ponderous or frail little fourteen-seaters which could not cope with increasing traffic requirements. The result was to take an existing Tilling-Stevens chassis and equip it with their own free-revving petrol engine and a four-speed gearbox and put this into production. Thus the SOS S type was born, and other BET operators realised that this bus was perhaps the answer to their prayers as well. Offered from 1924, when twenty-three S type chassis were sold, in 1925 another ninety-four were sold and by the time its successor, the SOS Q, was in full production in 1927, ninety-six chassis were sold. The peak year for sales was in 1928, when 179 QL buses and fifteen QLC coaches were sold. At the maximum the SOS chassis was purchased by nine operators. Perhaps it was significant that in the following year the AEC 'Regal' and the Leyland 'Tiger' were getting into production, both of which began to make inroads into the operators who were operating the SOS models. 119 vehicles were supplied in that year, but after that both the number of operators supplied and the number of vehicles sold gradually declined until by 1933 only Northern General, Potteries and Trent were buying vehicles from Midland Red. The British bus industry was producing more sophisticated vehicles by the mid-1930s which were less idiosyncratic than the products of the mainstream manufacturers. While the mid-1930s SOS was easy to drive and easy to maintain, it could not be provided in sufficient numbers by Carlyle Road Works. So from 1935 until production ended in 1940, only Trent Motor Traction purchased buses from BMMO, with fifteen double-decker FEDDs and 114 single-deckers.

Yet 1,000 chassis were purchased by BMMO for nine other operators in seventeen years, and many of the forward-control ones clocked up around twenty years of service. This was of course in addition to the buses built for 'home consumption'. So, far from being a 'bit' player, the SOS chassis were reliable and long-lived while being produced in much greater numbers than, for example, the products of Guy Motors and Maudslay, and only slightly less than Daimler.

The pre-war SOS therefore deserves a larger mention in the pantheon of British buses as it pioneered tram replacement buses which were fast, reliable and surprisingly long-lived and worth mentioning in the same breath as some of the larger bus manufacturers such as AEC and Leyland.

Endpiece

Any monogram or book about a particular bus manufacturer should have an endpiece which encapsulates the 'magic', idiosyncracies or uniqueness of that particular marque. Unfortunately, virtually every SOS bus built by the Birmingham & Midland Motor Omnibus Company between 1923 and 1940 automatically has all three of those characteristics. The choice of photograph at first sight might seem surprising, but it encapsulates everything 'quirky' about all the SOS models built for other operators. The bus is of a type that was built towards the end of the second generation of SOS chassis which had begun with the forward control FS and M types and so looked somewhat antiquated with an old-fashioned radiator and short length, round-topped bonnet that would not have looked out of place on a bus built five years earlier. Yet the body looks quite modern with deep side panels and radiused saloon windows. So the endpiece photograph is of an SOS type bus which is at a transition point in the development of PSV chassis to come out of Carlyle Road works in Edgbaston; it is owned by one of the smaller operators to whom the SOS chassis was supplied and looks a strange mixture of ancient and modern. *Magic, idiosyncratic AND unique!*

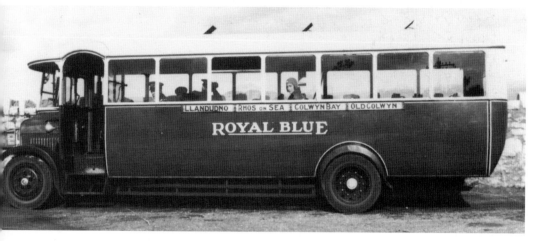

CC 8566
Llandudno Royal Blue's CC 8566 was a Ransomes, Simms & Jefferies-bodied SOS QL which seated thirty-four passengers. This bus had the SOS chassis number 1000. These were the last new SOS buses delivered to the operator as they were taken over by Crosville on 18 February 1931, an operator who did not favour the SOS marque. CC 8566 was the last of the six QLs delivered to Llandudno Royal Blue in 1929 and when taken over by Crosville was numbered 538, although it did not last long, being withdrawn in 1936. (D. R. Harvey Collection)

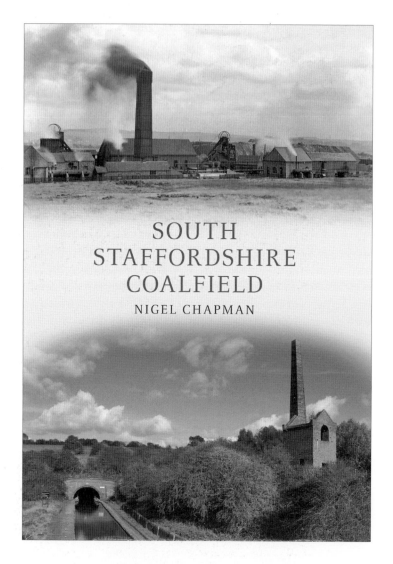

SOUTH
STAFFORDSHIRE
COALFIELD
NIGEL CHAPMAN

South Staffordshire Coalfield Through Time
Nigel Chapman

This fascinating selection of photographs traces some of the many
ways in which the South Staffordshire Coalfields have changed and
developed over the last century.

978 1 84868 971 8
96 pages, full colour

Available from all good bookshops or order direct
from our website www.amberleybooks.com